THE
TRUTH BEHIND
GHOSTS,
MEDIUMS &
PSYCHIC
PHENOMENA

RON RHODES

HARVEST HOUSE PUBLISHERS

EUGENE, OREGON

130
RHO

Cover by Terry Dugan Design, Minneapolis, Minnesota

Cover photo © Stockdisc / Stockdisc Premium / Getty Images

All emphasis in Scripture quotations is added by the author.

**THE TRUTH BEHIND GHOSTS, MEDIUMS, AND
PSYCHIC PHENOMENA**
Copyright © 2006 by Ron Rhodes
Published by Harvest House Publishers
Eugene, Oregon 97402

www.harvesthousepublishers.com

Library of Congress Cataloging-in-Publication Data
  Rhodes, Ron.
    The truth behind ghosts, mediums, and psychic phenomena / Ron Rhodes.
      p. cm.
  Includes bibliographical references and index.

  ISBN-13: 978-0-7369-1907-4 (pbk. : alk. paper)
  ISBN-10: 0-7369-1907-4 (alk. paper)

  1. Parapsychology. 2. Ghosts. 3. Mediums. I. Title.
  BF1031.R392 2006
  130--dc22
                  2006009772

Printed in the United States of America

06 07 08 09 10 11 12 13 14 / BP-SK / 10 9 8 7 6 5 4 3 2 1

TO GARY, PAT, MARSHA,
BRETT, MARK, AND RICK

ACKNOWLEDGMENTS

I want to express a heartfelt thanks to the leadership and staff at Harvest House Publishers for their continued willingness to publish relevant apologetics materials. I very much appreciate our partnership!

Thanks also to the elders at Frisco Bible Church, who provided much-needed prayer support while I wrote this book. I sometimes seemed to be in the midst of an all-out frontal assault from the powers of darkness that apparently intended to keep me from writing, but the prayers of the saints prevailed!

Finally, as always, I joyfully acknowledge my wife, Kerri, and our two children, David and Kylie, for their unceasing prayers and support. I praise the Lord for this wonderful family!

CONTENTS

CLOSE ENCOUNTERS WITH THE OTHER SIDE

PATRICIA AND ANDY POTTER
BATON ROUGE, LOUISIANA, 10:30 PM

Patricia and Andy put young Matthew to bed and watched a rerun of a popular sitcom. Andy had a job interview the next morning, so he didn't want to stay up too late.

About three and a half hours later, just after 2:00 AM, a noise woke Patricia. She bolted to Matthew's room to check on him, and he was sound asleep. *But what were those sounds?* They sounded like music coming from down the hall, in the playroom. Patricia could tell the lights were on in the room.

What on earth is going on? she wondered. She walked as quietly as she could, trying to avoid making the floor creak. She slowly turned the handle and, with deliberation, gently pushed the door open. Her eyes narrowed as she saw Matthew's toy carousel turning as it played music right in the middle of the floor. *I know everything was off and the lights were out when I went to bed,* Patricia thought.

Patricia turned off the carousel, flicked off the light switch, and went back to bed, still baffled at what she had seen. Nothing else unusual happened that night.

The next morning at breakfast, Patricia asked Matthew, "Did you leave any of your toys on last night before you went to bed?"

"Nope," he said.

When she told him one of his toys was on at 2:00 in the morning, he said maybe his special friend was playing with them.

"Special friend? What special friend?" she asked.

"Sometimes my special friend comes in the room," he said, "and we play together. I don't know his name or where he lives."

RICK HENDERSON
BROOKLYN, NEW YORK, 11:00 AM

Rick had been a churchgoer for years. Two months ago, his faith was shattered when Sarah died of cancer. They'd been married less than five years, and now she was gone. *Why would God let it happen?*

One Friday morning he pulled into the small parking lot of a local psychic named Mandy Blue. His appointment was for 11:00 AM.

Mandy was a middle-aged woman, unremarkable in appearance but quite friendly. She welcomed him to a chair in her office and began the session.

Mandy always preferred to spend the first 15 or 20 minutes of each one-hour session conversing with her client, getting a feel for his or her needs. She followed this with 30 minutes of attempting contact with dead loved ones. She reserved the last 10 minutes for any questions her client might have.

When she began conversing with Rick, she immediately sensed his heart was heavy. Rick informed her of his wife's passing and of his desire to communicate with her. His grief was debilitating, and he just had to talk to her.

Feeling a bit apprehensive, Rick asked her, "You're a Christian psychic, right?"

"That's right," Mandy said. "I believe my psychic ability is a gift of the Holy Spirit. And I use my psychic abilities to the glory of God."

"I don't want to do anything unchristian," Rick said, a concerned look on his face.

"I understand," Mandy said, smiling reassuringly. "And I appreciate your honesty. I know the Bible warns about false prophets, so we should be careful about these kinds of things. Why don't we begin, and we'll see if God will bless our session."

"Okay," Rick said. "What should I do?"

"Well, as I attune to the vibrational frequency of the spirit world, I just want you to interact with me and talk to me when I ask you a question so I can tell if I'm on target. I hope your wife will come through, but you need to be open-minded. Sometimes the people we seek do not come through, but someone else speaks instead—perhaps another relative or a friend who has crossed over to the Other Side. So if you're game, let's begin."

"Okay," Rick said.

Mandy put her fingers up to her temple and closed her eyes for a moment. Shortly thereafter, she opened her eyes, and her eyes narrowed. "I'm sensing a darkness or a shadow in the chest area. Was there some kind of cancer in the chest area?" she asked.

"Yes, Sarah died of breast cancer," Rick said.

"I'm sensing a piece of jewelry—a piece that is a closed circle," Mandy said. "Do you have perhaps a ring, a bracelet, or a necklace of Sarah's?"

"Yes," Rick said. "I put her wedding band on a necklace and wear it under my shirt."

"She knows that you do," Mandy said, "and she feels deep affection for you because of it." With compassion on her face, Mandy continued: "I'm sensing from Sarah that the main thing she wants you to know is that she is okay and that you shouldn't worry about her. Her love for you continues on the Other Side. I'm sensing that she wants you to live life to the fullest. When the day comes for you to cross over to the Other Side, she'll be waiting for you."

Rick involuntarily sobbed for a few moments.

He managed to regain his composure, and for the next few minutes he sat silently in the chair, staring at the floor. He sensed the session was coming to a close. He didn't have any remaining questions for Mandy, so he wrote her a check for the required fee of $400 and went home to reflect on Sarah's message through Mandy.

MARK AND AMY CHADWORTH
McMURPHY'S BED AND BREAKFAST
SEDONA, ARIZONA, 6:45 PM

Mark and Amy had been driving all day from Waco, Texas, en route to Anaheim, California, where they were going to visit Disneyland. This was going to be a vacation to remember!

Reaching Sedona, Arizona, they decided to call it a day. They intended to stay at a motel downtown, but they suddenly came upon McMurphy's Bed and Breakfast and decided on a whim to book a room there instead. After making the necessary arrangements with the owner, Mark hauled the luggage up to their room while Amy lingered behind to scope out the rest of the house.

Mark eyeballed the room and was impressed. They'd made a good choice. He specifically took notice of how nice the king-size bed looked. It was adorned with a beautiful Amish-made quilt and two large fluffy pillows. It looked comfortable. *Sleep would be nice tonight!*

He pulled a few things out of the suitcase and put them on the dresser. When he turned around again toward the bed, he froze. Moments before, the bed had been flat and smooth. Now one of the pillows had an indentation the exact size of someone's head, and the outline of a body was impressed on the quilt. The bed appeared as if someone invisible was lying on it.

A knock at the door startled Mark. He jolted toward the door and yanked it open. As soon as Amy saw his face, she said, "Honey, what is it? You look like you've seen a ghost." Mark grabbed her hand and dragged her toward the bed, which was now perfectly smooth. No indention whatsoever. Mark ran his hands up and down the surface of the bed with a look of bewilderment on his face. When he explained what had happened, Amy looked incredulous, laughed, and said, "Honey, you just need a good night of sleep." Mark's jaw muscle twitched. He scratched his head.

They went to bed at about 11:00. Though Mark saw nothing else out of the ordinary during the night, he felt ill-at-ease. *Was some kind of presence in the room?* He slept fitfully all night, often sitting up to look around the room. He couldn't wait to leave the place.

At breakfast the next morning, to Amy's chagrin, Mark brought the subject up with Mrs. McMurphy, who was serving eggs, sausage, and French toast. Mark put a macho light spin on the experience, pretending they'd been amused at the idea of an invisible visitor. Without blinking an eye, Mrs. McMurphy responded, "Oh, maybe you saw the ghost of my great-great-grandmother Emma. She died in her sleep in that very room many years ago."

LEE AND GRACE CLANCY
LOS ANGELES, CALIFORNIA, 1:00 PM

Lee and Grace pulled into the driveway of a house at the end of a cul-de-sac. A medium who often advertised in the local Penny Saver tabloid lived here. Her name was Penny Watts.

Lee had made an appointment with her because he was in the midst of an emotional downward spiral. He struggled with feelings of severe guilt and depression. He was tormented by his mother's death.

Six months earlier, Lee had driven to his mother's house and found her unconscious. He rushed her to the emergency room, and shortly thereafter, doctors informed him that his mother had suffered a severe stroke in her brain. Because of oxygen deprivation, the monitors showed no brain activity. Life-support equipment was keeping the rest of her body alive.

During the next week, she remained in this condition without change. Lee prayed and hoped for a miracle, but her condition did not improve. She lay perfectly still with a breathing tube down her throat, an intravenous tube attached to her arm, and various wires attaching her body to monitors. He held her hand and talked to her. "Mom, what should I do?"

His mother was eventually transferred out of the intensive care unit to one of the regular rooms upstairs in the hospital. Nurses carefully monitored her condition. Things remained the same for the next several weeks. The doctors began hinting that Lee would soon need to make some difficult decisions.

A short time later, after talking with his wife, some trusted friends, and a local minister, Lee made the hard decision to withdraw life support from his brain-dead mother.

It was over all too quickly. Minutes after the life-support equipment was turned off, she was gone. Her heart stopped beating. Her lungs stopped breathing. Lee hugged her as he wept.

From that moment forward, he struggled with severe feelings of guilt over his decision. Would a miracle have happened if he had waited just one more week? Would his mother now be alive if he hadn't instructed the doctors to pull the plug? Did he make the wrong choice? Did he make the choice too soon?

To make matters worse, some of his mother's relatives had not accepted Lee's decision. Months passed. His guilt grew increasingly burdensome.

Penny Watts, the medium, welcomed Lee and Grace into her home, and they all took a seat in a parlor room. Lee explained everything about his mother, and Penny seemed truly empathetic. She expressed willingness to do anything she could to help.

The session began. Penny closed her eyes for a few moments as she attuned to the spirit world. She looked Lee in the eyes and said with reassurance, "I sense two female spirits above you. They are in your family line, both older than you. Has your grandmother also passed over to the Other Side?"

"Yes," Lee said. "She died of a heart attack years ago."

"Okay," Penny said. "They're both here with you."

Lee started to tear up.

"I'm also sensing a father figure along with your mother and grandmother. Has your father passed over?"

"Yes," Lee said.

"He died recently, didn't he?" Penny asked.

"No, he died about seven years ago," Lee said.

"Okay," Penny conceded.

"He died of a heart attack?" Penny asked.

"No," Lee said, eyes narrowing. "He died of lung cancer."

"Okay, things seem a little fuzzy about your father. Don't worry." Penny paused for a moment. She then said, "I strongly sense your mother coming through, seeking to communicate to you that everything is okay. She wants you to stop feeling guilty and to realize you did everything you could. She is at peace and wants you to be at peace. All is well."

Lee wept quietly as Grace embraced him.

They all sat silently for a few minutes. The session had come to a close.

"Lee, I feel good about this. Don't you?" Penny asked.

Lee nodded.

He wrote her a check to cover the required $250 fee for the half-hour session and left with Grace.

KAREN AND GARY HOLMES
SEATTLE, WASHINGTON, 3:23 AM

"I bolted upright in my bed. A primal fear gripped my heart. I felt a sense of sudden panic, but I'm not sure why. I thought I heard something. *Did I?*

"My heart was beating way too fast. Something was desperately wrong. I froze in place.

"I wanted to breathe deeply, but I was so afraid—so intent on listening, so desiring not to be discovered by some unknown intruder—that I breathed quietly, deliberately. In the process, my slowed breathing began to starve my lungs for the oxygen they so craved at this fearful moment. But I dared not breathe any faster or louder for fear of being discovered.

"Why is my room so cold? And what is that smell?

"'Gary,' I tried to say, wanting to wake my husband. I was unable to speak. My voice was choked by fear. My panic increased. I felt paralyzed—utterly petrified. *What is happening?*

"A deeper, suffocating fear descended on me as I started to sense I was being watched. It was an intuitive feeling. I could sense some kind of presence near me. I remained frozen and waited in silence. *I needed to breathe.*

"My peripheral vision suddenly detected motion to my left, where the bedroom door opens into the hallway. *Please God, help me.* Did somebody—*something*—just pass by the door?

"I stared into the darkness, my heart racing and pounding, my lungs screaming for oxygen. I was fearful of even blinking my eyes. I instinctively pulled the cover up closer to my face. 'Gary,' I tried to say again. My voice, still choked by fear, remained silent.

"A car suddenly turned on a street nearby, and its headlight briefly illuminated the room. My throat constricted as I saw a hooded figure in a dark robe standing in the hallway, peering into the bedroom. This person—*this thing, this predator that seemed to emanate evil*—was simply standing there, staring. I didn't see a face, but whatever was beneath that hood seemed hollow, maybe even transparent.

"I had no time to analyze things, no time to devise a plan of action. With a rush of adrenaline charging through my veins, I screamed at the top of my lungs. Gary jerked violently, swung to the right, knocked everything off the night table, jolted to flip on the lamp, and looked at me with imploring eyes.

"'What happened?' he begged.

"I couldn't answer. Holding the covers up close to my face, I was crying. I was staring at the open doorway, and the figure was gone. He—*it*—had vanished."

The stories you have just read are fictional. But when I wrote them, I made sure they were faithful to the kinds of things real-life people claim to have experienced.[1] These people are convinced they've had a close encounter with the Other Side.

Such wild stories are more common than you might think. I've encountered virtually hundreds of such stories as I've conducted research for this book.

Based on my research, I think I am safe in saying that in some sectors of our society, the paranormal has become the new normal. Indeed, tens of millions of people have rejected Christianity and replaced it with belief in ghosts, spirit guides, psychic phenomena, out-of-body experiences, and the like. Psychics are currently communicating messages from these spirit entities that blatantly contradict the teachings of the Bible.

Christians need not be afraid. But neither should we ignore the rise of these strange phenomena. Instead, we can take a hard look at what is going on and find out what the Bible has to say about it. I therefore invite you to strap on your seat belt and join me in a journey through the strange world of the paranormal and the occult. By the time we are finished, you'll have a much heightened awareness of what is *really* going on in our society—and who is behind it!

ONE

PARANORMAL: THE NEW NORMAL?

The paranormal has become the new normal among certain sectors of the religious demographic in America. A recent Gallup poll, for example, reveals that 32 percent of Americans believe in some sort of paranormal activity.[1] The same poll reveals that 38 percent of Americans believe ghosts or spirits can come back and visit us. Twenty-eight percent of Americans think people can communicate with or "mentally" talk to the dead.[2]

Spiritism—the belief that the dead communicate with the living—is no longer confined to the periphery of our society. No longer is occultism a fringe idea. Brooks Alexander, a cofounder of the Spiritual Counterfeits Project in Berkeley, California, suggests that "spiritism has moved beyond the weird and the supernatural into the normal and the mundane. Quietly, but convincingly, the entities [that is, spirits from the Other Side] have been serving notice that they intend to shape our future."[3]

Bill O'Reilly, of *The O'Reilly Factor,* says life after death is big business today. "It is a huge business in America—books, tapes, lectures—and 65 percent of Americans say they do believe in an afterlife."[4] Unfortunately, this interest in the afterlife has led many to seek contact with those on the Other Side. In keeping with this escalating interest, psychic John Edward—not to be confused with politician

John Edwards—had a television show, *Crossing Over,* in syndication on 210 TV stations, blanketing 98 percent of the United States.[5] As well, over the past decade, today's primetime psychic mediums— John Edward, James Van Praagh, and Sylvia Browne—have appeared on *Larry King Live* at least 20 times.[6] Browne has also been a weekly regular on *The Montel Williams Show.*[7]

One might be tempted to think only uneducated people believe in such ideas. This is not the case, however. A study conducted by Bryan Farha of Oklahoma City University and Gary Steward Jr. of the University of Central Oklahoma found that as students progress through their college years, they become more likely to believe in paranormal concepts. More specifically, they found that while 23 percent of freshmen believe in paranormal concepts, 31 percent of seniors and 34 percent of graduate students believe in such concepts.[8]

Many of today's college professors believe in extrasensory perception, often associated with the paranormal. A survey of 1100 college professors found that 34 percent of psychologists, 55 percent of natural scientists, 66 percent of other social scientists, and 77 percent of professors in the humanities believed in extrasensory perception as an established fact or a likely possibility.[9]

The paranormal has made huge inroads among our nation's teenagers. In early 2006, George Barna conducted a poll that revealed that 73 percent of America's youth have participated in psychic activities and/or witchcraft. Four out of five have had their horoscopes read by an astrologer. One-third have played with a Ouija board or read a book about witchcraft, or Wicca. More than one-fourth have played occultic games. One-tenth have participated in a séance, attempting to contact the dead. One-twelfth have attempted to cast spells or mix magic potions. Thirty percent have participated in palm reading, and 27 percent have had their fortune told.[10]

Barna also discovered that seven million teenagers claim to have personally encountered a spirit entity, such as an angel, a demon, or some other supernatural entity. Two million claim to have psychic powers. And amazingly, among churchgoing teen-agers, only 28 percent say they've been taught anything at church to help shape their views of the supernatural world.[11]

The Paranormal in Hollywood

The paranormal seems to have nearly taken over Hollywood. One indication of this is that networks produced 14 pilots with supernatural themes for the 2005–2006 TV season. Movies are also brimming with the paranormal. The *Johns Hopkins Newsletter* suggests, "One only has to look at the popularity of documentaries, television programs, books, and films that explore the world of ghosts to see a public devoted to the paranormal."[12]

PARANORMAL TV SHOWS

Medium is a very popular TV show. This drama features a woman, played by Patricia Arquette, who is a research medium for an Arizona district attorney's office. She can allegedly talk to dead people, see the future in her dreams, and read people's thoughts. She uses her "gifts" to solve violent and horrifying crimes.

Ghost Whisperer, another series, stars Jennifer Love Hewitt. She plays a woman who helps dead people deliver messages to living loved ones, thereby enabling them to finally find peace on the Other Side. In an interview, Hewitt said she finds the Hollywood Forever Cemetery a soothing place to visit: "I wonder who these people were, how they died, and what their stories were…I look at them hoping they are at peace and didn't have any unfinished business."[13]

Herein lies a key premise of *Ghost Whisperer.* The ghosts Hewitt interacts with on the show cling to the living because they allegedly have unfinished business that prevents them from moving on with their existence in the great beyond. Hewitt seeks to help the people she meets—whether alive or dead—find emotional closure. In one episode, a little boy who died because he disobeyed his mother refused to move on until she told him he was forgiven. By the end of the show, the viewing audience feels uplifted and comforted about this communication between the living and the dead. The show really pulls on the heartstrings. Hewitt says people worry that when they die, "it's all over and you don't get a say in it. We try to say in our show that maybe you go on to something new."[14]

While researching her role, Hewitt had a psychic reading with the famous psychic medium James Van Praagh. Hewitt believes she was able to make contact with her friend Allen, who died when she was just 12 years old.

Interestingly, *The Hollywood Reporter* reveals that the producer of *Ghost Whisperer*, John Gray, had no experiences with the paranormal—at least until he was shooting the pilot for the new show:

> Gray was just getting settled into a new home in New York when he, his fiancée, and his daughter began hearing noises in the house—such as the sounds of furniture moving around in the attic or someone walking up and down stairs. Lights would turn on at random, and in one instance, an entire set of puzzle pieces overturned by itself.[15]

Gray says, "It was the closest experience with the supernatural I've had of any kind."[16] He ended up utilizing the services of a medium who serves as a consultant on the show, and she informed him that two spirits were living in the house who liked the previous owners better than Gray and his family. The medium allegedly persuaded the spirits to "cross over." Since then, the hauntings have ceased. (I will biblically evaluate such claims later in the book.)

Does Gray believe in ghosts now? "I try to be open-minded—it's arrogant to say it's impossible...There's more out there than we are aware of, and there are things that we can't explain. I certainly hope it's true."[17]

James Van Praagh is one force behind this current plethora of paranormal shows. The *New York Daily News* uses this clever play on words:

> Psychic James Van Praagh has always made a nice living by claiming to see dead people. But he has made a killing

with his ability to foresee how television audiences would be entranced by programming about psychic phenomena, haunted houses, and other otherworldly encounters. He's channeling a trend that has ghost-themed shows materializing on several, well, channels.[18]

Van Praagh, author of a number of bestselling books on communicating with spirit entities, is an executive producer of *Ghost Whisperer*. Many of the show's episodes are based on real-life cases taken from his files. He boasts that he predicted the rise of interest in psychic phenomena some years ago on *Larry King Live*, right after the release of the blockbuster movie *The Sixth Sense*. "What's so amazing," he says, "is how it's become much more acceptable in the mainstream, where you're now seeing more and more of these types of shows."[19] He says the TV landscape has become a veritable ghost town in recent years—meaning that interest in ghosts is everywhere in Hollywood.

Another popular TV show is *Ghost Hunters*, which is aired on the Sci-Fi Channel. This reality series features a team of paranormal investigators from Rhode Island who travel to supposedly haunted sites throughout the United States and attempt to garner evidence of ghostly activity. These investigators utilize high-tech equipment like infrared cameras and digital recorders. Dave Tango, one of the stars of *Ghost Hunter*, makes this claim:

> There's no doubt in my mind that there is something there. There is some other plane on earth where they exist… Right now, all we have is some weird energy and occurrences we can't explain, but I believe that will change in a few years. I believe, in a few years, we will be able to prove scientifically that ghosts exist.[20]

Yet another TV show is *Dead Tenants*, airing on The Learning Channel. In this show, psychics, spiritual intuitives, ghost chasers, and occult specialists help homeowners with unwanted ghost problems and other unexplainable activity. One psychic on the show says, "It's not that we are trying to get rid of the ghosts…We are more like social workers. We see why [the spirits] are there."[21] For homeowners who feel they have been harassed by ghosts, the paranormal investigators engage in a special "cleansing" ritual that allegedly puts the spirits at peace.

In keeping with this wave of interest in the paranormal, The Biography Channel airs a reality show called *Dead Famous: Ghostly Encounters*. This show pairs a female skeptic with a male psychic as they chase after the spirits of such deceased famous folks as Frank Sinatra, Marilyn Monroe, and Jim Morrison.

Even The Travel Channel has gotten in on ghostly phenomena, featuring the popular *America's Most Haunted Places* and *Haunted Hotels*. The show features a team of paranormal investigators who travel to various sites throughout Europe in search of ghosts.

Court TV features a popular show called *Psychic Detectives,* which recounts real-life cases in which cops and psychics work together. The success of this show has motivated Court TV to debut another show entitled *Haunting Evidence,* which pairs a psychic, a medium, and a forensics expert who visit various haunted crime scenes. By joining their efforts, they seek to bring fresh insight to "cold cases" and perhaps help bring closure to the families of victims.

One final TV show worthy of mention is *Ghost Trackers,* airing in Canada. In this reality TV show, kids compete to become the ultimate "ghost master" by investigating paranormal activity in a variety of haunted venues. The winners move on to subsequent competitions.[22]

Why are such TV shows so popular? Van Praagh offers this suggestion: "More people than ever are believing in life after death. They're looking for other belief systems and for other ways to deal with the world around them, and people want to find out what this is all about."[23]

PARANORMAL MOVIES

The paranormal has also been quite popular in major motion pictures. Though many dozens of films have featured ghosts throughout Hollywood history, *Poltergeist* brought the paranormal into the mainstream consciousness of America.

Polter is the German word for "noisy" or "rumbling." *Geist* is the German word for "ghost" or "spirit." Hence, *poltergeist* refers to a "noisy ghost" or "noisy spirit"—a spirit that disrupts households by moving and influencing inanimate objects. The movie, produced by Steven Spielberg in the 1980s, portrays a family being terrorized by a poltergeist infestation in a house built over a graveyard.

Ghost was another hugely popular paranormal movie. Patrick Swayze plays a young man who is suddenly ripped out of his physical body but stays on earth long enough to solve the mystery of his murder. He seeks to reconnect with his girlfriend, played by Demi Moore, and in the process, educates both himself and the viewing audience to the "realities" of being a real-live ghost.

A cover story in *Body, Mind & Spirit* (New Age) magazine features an interview with the movie's writer and director, Bruce Joel Rubin. He says, "*Ghost* has made it big because it reawakens us powerfully and passionately to who we really are as multidimensional beings. Its depiction of death and the astral world breathes magic back into our daily lives."[24] Occultists believe the astral world is a spiritual dimension or level of being that lies just beyond the physical world. (I'll talk more about this later in the book.) *Ghost* was one of the top-grossing films of all time and has been an incredibly powerful promotional vehicle for the paranormal.

In *The Sixth Sense*, Haley Joel Osment plays a troubled, isolated boy who claims to see dead people. By the end of the movie, the boy tries to help some of these dead people deal with unresolved problems so they can be at peace. The movie earned more than $293 million in the United States and a worldwide gross of $672 million, making it number 22 on the list of biggest money-making movies of all time. The line "I see dead people" became a popular catchphrase after the film's release. Famous psychic Sylvia Browne, her psychic son, Chris, and her psychic seven-year-old granddaughter, Angelia, went to see the movie, and Browne commented, "We appreciated how accurately one of our daily realities was portrayed."[25]

White Noise was yet another hit movie. When a radio or TV is on but not tuned to a channel, one hears "white noise." Occultists believe spirits can communicate with living people through white noise. This form of communication from the beyond is known as EVP—Electronic Voice Phenomenon. In the movie, an architect named Jonathan grieves over the recent death of his wife. A paranormal expert then approaches Jonathan with an unusual claim: the ability to hear his wife from beyond the grave through white noise. Jonathan subsequently becomes obsessed with using electronic equipment to contact his wife in the great beyond.

One final paranormal movie worthy of mention is *The Ring*. In this movie, the spirit of a little girl who was murdered terrorizes and kills other people. Any character in the movie who watches a particular video receives a phone call that says they have seven days, and then they are violently killed seven days later. The dead girl's body is eventually discovered at the bottom of a well, and she is given a proper burial. But instead of being put to rest, the spirit is more interested in continuing to harm the living. The only way to escape harm is to make a copy of the tape and show it to someone else.

Cultural analysts have debated whether TV shows and films *shape* peoples' beliefs or merely *reflect* them. Perhaps both are true. On the one hand, movie producer George Lucas once commented that TV shows and films are teachers with very loud voices. Certainly Hollywood productions have introduced many people to the world of the paranormal. On the other hand, such TV shows and films may be successful because the target market is already so huge.

CELEBRITY CLIENTS FOR PSYCHICS

Stars who openly utilize the services of psychics have also given a PR boost to the paranormal. For example, many newspapers and tabloids reported James Van Praagh's alleged contact of O.J. Simpson's murdered wife, Nicole Brown Simpson, on behalf of her sister, Denise Brown.[26] The famous singer Cher also utilized Van Praagh's psychic talents in allegedly communicating with her late ex-husband, Sonny Bono, shortly after he died in a bizarre skiing accident at Lake Tahoe in 1998.[27] Van Praagh's clientele has also included the late Audrey Meadows, who believed that through him she was able to make contact with her dead TV husband, Jackie Gleason.[28] Interestingly, many years ago I had the opportunity of doing a TV talk show with Gleason, and I remember him commenting that he owned one of the largest private occult libraries in the world.

Government Interest in the Paranormal

Even the United States government has been interested in the occult and the paranormal. According to government documents that were declassified in the 1990s, the United States—during the years of America's cold war with the Soviet Union—spent a whopping $20 million studying extrasensory perception and other psychic phenomena "in an effort to determine whether these forces of the paranormal world could somehow be put to use by espionage experts in the natural world."[29] (The $20 million was wasted.)

Former president Jimmy Carter once consulted a psychic to do what the United States' satellite surveillance system couldn't do—find a downed American plane in Africa. Carter recalls the experience:

> We had a plane go down in the Central African Republic—a twin-engine plane, small plane. And we couldn't find it. So we oriented satellites that were going around the earth every 90 minutes to fly over that spot where we thought it might be and take photographs. We couldn't find it. So the director of the CIA (Stansfield Turner) came and told me that he had contacted a woman in California that claimed to have supernatural capabilities. And she went into a trance, and she wrote down latitudes and longitudes, and we sent our satellites over that latitude and longitude, and there was the plane.[30]

Paranormal Education

Today the various means of becoming educated in paranormal and psychic phenomena seem to have no end. In fact, paranormal education has become big business.

COMMUNITY COLLEGE COURSES

One can take a variety of courses on the paranormal from local community colleges. In one newspaper we read, "Want to learn how to develop your psychic abilities?...Look no further than your local community college, where a variety of unusual non-credit courses are being offered."[31] The school also offers courses on ghosts and how to contact the dead.

A GHOST SCHOOL IN THE UNITED KINGDOM

A new school for ghost hunters was established in 2006 in the United Kingdom. Dr. Jason Braithwaite teaches students the scientific skills needed to investigate "haunted" houses in a two-day course at Muncaster Castle. This castle is well known for spine-chilling manifestations of spooks and specters. In this building, "sounds of children crying and screaming, feelings of another-worldly presence, the sound of footsteps, and fleeting visions have all been reported."[32] Braithwaite, a cognitive psychologist and neuroscientist from the University of Birmingham, seeks to teach people the skills they will need to decide for themselves what lies behind such strange phenomena.

A PARANORMAL E-MAIL COURSE

A six-week course for developing psychic intuition is available online. The course claims to "shatter the mystery about psychic phenomena and makes the intuitive world accessible to anyone."[33]

GHOST SEMINARS

Seminars across the United States teach people about paranormal phenomena and hunting for ghosts. One such seminar in

Aspen, Colorado, taught attendees how to use cameras to capture ghost orbs on film and how to use meters to measure electrical activity inside a building, thereby (allegedly) indicating the presence of a paranormal being. (A "ghost orb" is allegedly a ghostly sphere of light that represents the soul of a dead person.) One of the leaders at this seminar made this comment:

> The one thing I found from the spirits here is that the majority seem very content. The majority of them have already moved on. They can go back and forth, and sometimes they come back to places that are fond memories for them.[34]

I will biblically evaluate this idea later in the book.

Psychic Fairs

Psychic fairs have also become very popular in our day. At such fairs, psychics often give readings to attendees and help them communicate with friends or relatives who have died, or crossed over to the Other Side. Other psychics give tarot card readings for people. In some cases, psychics offer to take photographs of people's psychic auras and interpret them (more on this later in the book). Through such fairs, many people have been introduced to the world of occultism.[35]

Paranormal Weekends

Similar to the psychic fair, some people like to attend "paranormal weekends." During such weekends, skeptics and believers alike are invited to listen to lectures about paranormal investigation. At some of these events, speakers teach attendees how to use special photographic equipment to photograph ghost orbs. After brief training, attendees are invited to visit different areas and attempt to take their own photographs of ghost orbs. By attending such paranormal weekends, a person can become certified in paranormal investigation.[36]

Other Paranormal Promotions

Today many games are on the market that are rooted in the paranormal. Such games are often played in the dark, involve various occultic activities, and can have unexpected, even terrifying results.[37] Popular games include Light as a Feather—Stiff as a Board, Ouija, Bloody Mary, and bending spoons. Sometimes teens sneak into abandoned or allegedly haunted buildings at night and play these games.

Teens like these games for the same reason they like horror movies—they like to be scared. Understandably, most researchers recommend that people avoid such games. Let us consider two examples:

The game Light as a Feather—Stiff as a Board is a levitation game. In this game, one person lies on the ground, and four people sit around him or her. Each of the four place two fingers of each hand beneath the body and began chanting, "light as a feather... stiff as a board..." With hardly any effort, the four are able to raise the person off the floor in apparent defiance of gravity. While many consider this activity benign, some researchers warn that levitation is part and parcel of the world of the occult.

Another example is Ouija, a game board containing numbers and letters with a pointer that a "visiting spirit" can use to communicate a message from the Other Side by guiding the hand of the players. Participants ask questions, and the pointer seems to magically slide around the board, spelling different words. The Ouija board can be purchased in just about any mainstream toy store. Tragically, teenagers who play this game are completely unaware that they are opening themselves up to the world of the occult, often with terrifying consequences.

Several radio shows focus exclusively on the paranormal. For example, in the Twin Cities in Minnesota, one radio talk show focuses on ghosts, hauntings, and UFOs. The show is called "The Darkness on the Edge of Town" and features local and national guests. One of the first guests was the lead investigator and star of the Sci-Fi Channel's *Ghost Hunters* TV show.[38]

Another paranormal radio show is the "Kevin Smith Show," now broadcast in 53 countries via the Globalstar Communications Network. Smith says, "My guests are hot and the topics are sizzling. People are interested in the strange and unexplained."[39]

The BBC reports that the Ultraviolet Insurance Company has written a policy for a store that will pay out up to one million pounds "if staff or customers are killed or suffer permanent disability caused by ghosts, poltergeists, or other abnormal phenomena on the premises."[40]

A recent book titled *Above Us Only Sky: A View of 9/11 from the Spirit World* gives accounts of 9/11 that are communicated from dead people. This book, written by medium Sarah Price, is comprised of channeled messages from deceased victims of 9/11 and from "spirit witnesses" who saw the entire event unfold. These spirit witnesses include Anne Frank, President John F. Kennedy, John Lennon, and NBC journalist David Bloom, "who bring their own insights on the events of 9/11 and advice on life in general."[41]

This chapter shows the prevalence of psychic phenomena among teenagers, college students, college professors, and the general adult population in the United States. It also demonstrates the paranormal's influence in Hollywood and summarizes some occult educational opportunities. It has provided a brief taste of the more wacky side of ghostly phenomena.

I think you can now see why I believe the paranormal has become the new normal in some sectors of America's religious landscape. In the next chapter, we will focus attention on the appeal of the paranormal in our day.

TWO

UNDERSTANDING THE APPEAL

Interest in ghosts and contacting the dead were once relegated mainly to fringe cultic groups. But not anymore. Ghosts and spiritism have infiltrated the popular culture—big time. Belief in paranormal phenomena is soaring across the religious spectrum in America.

One must therefore ask, why has the paranormal become the new normal for so many Americans? Why have psychics become so intensely popular? Why have tens of millions in our society become interested in contacting the dead? *What is the appeal?*

I wish the answer to this question were simple—like looking at a single item with a telescope. The truth in this case is more like a kaleidoscope, with many factors contributing to the popularity of paranormal phenomena in our society.

An Invasion of Eastern Philosophy

The 1960s brought a massive invasion of Eastern philosophy into the West. This openness to Eastern religion was largely a reaction against traditional Western values, including high technology, reason and rationalism, materialism, capitalism, and the like.

Eastern philosophy, with its antirationalism, quietism, and lack of technology, appealed to many.

Some religious analysts believe the current interest in contacting the dead may be a spillover doctrine from the emergence of Eastern spirituality in the 1960s. Because of Eastern influence, many people today are much more open to the unseen. As one analyst said, "Spirits, whatever their nature, are utterly fascinating to people who once believed that the physical universe was all that existed."[1] One can certainly detect heavy Eastern influence—including belief in reincarnation and the law of karma—in the writings of some of today's prime-time psychics, including James Van Praagh, John Edward, Sylvia Browne, and Char Margolis.

Burned-Out on Traditional Religion

Unfortunately, some people have become interested in occultism and paranormal phenomena simply because they are burned-out on traditional religion. Many who have attended church in the past feel that the church is lifeless and has not met real needs. They believe the church has become irrelevant to modern society. Van Praagh says that "people are searching. Boomers are questioning their own destinies. Organized religion is not answering these simple questions."[2]

Such people are in search of a spirituality that works. The idea that all people, regardless of what religion they subscribe to, survive death and cross over to the Other Side—and can still communicate with us—is a religious belief system that "works" for many people.

Several of today's prime-time psychics became burned-out on Catholicism before becoming psychics. In fact, Van Praagh claims he was mistreated by some of the nuns at his Catholic school. He recalls, "I didn't have the right colored pencil for a lesson, so Sister Matilda slapped me—so hard that I went flying to the floor and lost a moment of consciousness."[3] He says he witnessed firsthand a distance between what his Catholic teachers preached and what they demonstrated.[4]

Much later, Van Praagh burned out on the doctrines he was taught at a Catholic prep seminary, which he attended primarily to please his mother. He came to dislike the judgmentalism he saw in the church. "I could no longer believe in a mythology that centered on guilt and punishment."[5] He recalls, "Church didn't make sense. They talked about loving God, but then they judged people. By opening up to spirits, my sense of religion ended, but my sense of spirituality began."[6] Contrary to a God who judges and sends some people to hell, Van Praagh increasingly came to believe that God is permeated by love, is virtually nonjudgmental, and is manifested within every human being.[7] He therefore left the seminary and said goodbye to the Catholic church.

Sylvia Browne is another primetime psychic who burned out on Catholicism. She recalls her sixth-grade class studying about hell, Satan, and the possibility of being possessed by Satan. This was not a version of Christianity that appealed to her. This version of Christianity was the stuff nightmares were made of. "It made no sense to me that the God who created and loved us from the bottom of His perfect heart could also be so cold, cruel, and hateful that He would doom us to an eternity in hell if we ate meat on Friday [a Catholic prohibition during her childhood], or even harbored a sinful thought, whether we acted on it or not."[8]

Browne also had serious problems with the idea of confessing sins to a priest. "If I needed an intermediary between me and God, why bother to pray, unless that same priest is around to pass messages back and forth?"[9] She also wondered why, if God loves every person equally, He would pay more attention to a priest than to her?

Still further, Browne expressed great dissatisfaction with the Christian doctrine of the afterlife. She could not understand how, after just one lifetime on earth, a person would be consigned by God to either heaven or hell for all eternity.[10] The theology of the spirits—including the doctrine of reincarnation—would eventually make much more sense to her.

Some Psychics Sound Christian

Some Christians may feel inclined to visit psychics because some of them actually sound Christian. John Edward claims to be a Catholic and even prays the rosary prior to his psychic readings.[11] Char Margolis claims her psychic gift is God-given.[12] Sylvia Browne often refers to God, Christ, and the Holy Spirit during her television appearances. She claims to do all that she does by the grace of God. Her website claims "the Holy Spirit works through Sylvia to emanate God's love, grace, and blessings."[13] All this sounds very Christian!

A look at these psychics' theology, however, clearly shows that they are not *biblical* Christians. They apparently fail to perceive— or they choose to ignore—that their involvement in psychic phenomena is a violation of God's commandments.

An Experience-Oriented Society

Today we are living in experiential times. People place a lot of stock in feelings: "If it feels good, it must be right." "How can it be wrong if it feels so right?" Rather than embracing an objective, factually-based faith, resting on divine authority, many today are seeking mystical and emotional experience.[14] We might say that the paranormal is the experiential flavor of the day. Powerful experiences associated with the occult and the paranormal are forceful persuaders that a spiritual world exists and that people can contact this spiritual world.

One of the reasons for the success of John Edward's *Crossing Over* TV show is that it touched the human heart. One analyst noted, "Edward manages to traverse the range of human emotions deftly in 30 minutes, piloting us from grief and fear to hope and joy to, inevitably, redemption and closure. Not only does the audience usually cry at some point during the process, but the staff often tears up as well."[15]

Another analyst noted that Edward "connects with people on an emotional level, and it's very compelling...Even if you're totally skeptical, you can't ignore that a lot of people in the studio audience are experiencing something, whether it's what they bring or what he provides, and that's what makes it great TV."[16]

Related to this, many religious observers have noted that people who seek contact with the dead really *want* to believe. They are so desirous of making contact with dead loved ones, whom they grievously miss, that they become emotionally invested in the success of their session with a psychic medium. Even if the psychic medium gets some facts wrong, they are still emotionally committed to (and desperately hoping for) some genuine contact with dead loved ones.

Fascination with the Supernatural

Certainly one reason for the popularity of psychic phenomena is that some people are fascinated with all things supernatural. This is especially true with many of today's teenagers who play with Ouija boards and various paranormal games. Many people who are fascinated with paranormal phenomena and who participate in psychic readings and séances think these are benign activities that make for an exciting thrill. Such people are often unaware of the Bible's condemnation of such activities.

People Want to Know the Future

Many people are interested in psychics' alleged ability to read the future. These seekers sometimes feel insecure, but more often they simply want to know what lies just around the corner. For example, a person might go to a psychic to find out whether or not a particular romantic relationship will last. A person might go to a psychic to ascertain whether he or she has a good future with a particular company. Or a person might go to a psychic to become aware of—and then avoid—any dangers in his or her future. Many feel that having this inside knowledge gives them an edge when making decisions for their lives. (I will demonstrate later in the book how utterly inaccurate psychics are in reading the future.)

Curiosity About the Other Side

All people die. The current statistics indicate that three people die in the world every second, 180 every minute, and nearly 11,000 every hour. This means that about 250,000 people die each and every day.[17] Understandably, people are curious to know about what happens after death. In view of this interest, psychic Sylvia Browne tries to comfort her readers by telling them, "The Other Side is reality, as real as the ground we walk on, the bodies our spirits inhabit, and the air we breathe. And the truth about the Other Side is more thrilling, comforting, loving, and empowering than any fairy tale could ever be."[18] Contrary to the Bible, psychics assure us that regardless of what religion people subscribe to, everyone crosses over to an enjoyable existence on the Other Side.

Communication with Dead Loved Ones

In view of the perpetual reality of death, tens of millions of people today want to do anything they can to engage in communication with their dead loved ones. This is the single most important reason for the popularity of psychics today. Related to this, my former colleague Walter Martin, in his book *The Kingdom of the Cults*, said that "spiritism has made its strongest appeal to those who have suffered great loss, and after each great war, spiritism always seems to be on the upgrade following the death of loved ones."[19] Tragically, many turn to spiritism instead of the Bible for comfort.

Many people are interested in contacting their dead loved ones because today's psychics are feeding them the lie that their dead loved ones are *already* trying to make contact with them. Van Praagh makes this claim:

> Once acclimated to their new world, spirits begin to hear our thoughts of grief, sadness, and regret. They see the pain and anguish brought on by their death. Knowing that they are still alive, albeit in another form, they want to reassure us that they are still aware of everything taking place on earth...

Depending upon a spirit's personality, abilities, and its own awareness, it will attempt in every way possible to communicate and get us to understand its newly relocated existence.[20]

Answers to the Deeper Questions of Life

Some people believe that spiritism—the belief that the dead communicate with the living—offers answers to some of the deeper questions of life. For example, many reason that if spiritism is true, then this life must have a spiritual dimension, and people can look forward to an afterlife as well. And since psychics say people of all religions are equally welcome in the afterlife, one need not be a Christian to look forward to the joys of heaven. In view of all this, people conclude they have no legitimate reason to fear death.

Following Parents' Footsteps

One reason young people become involved in occultism and the paranormal is that their parents have already long been involved in such practices. Children are sometimes conditioned from early childhood to accept paranormal phenomena. For example, psychic Sylvia Browne was exposed to psychic phenomena as a child by her grandmother. Sylvia's son, Chris, apparently became a psychic due to her own influence. Chris's daughter, Angelia, is also a psychic. John Edward's mother often invited psychics to their home to do readings.

Peer Pressure

Some teenagers participate in séances, play with Ouija boards, play paranormal games, and experiment with various other forms of occultism only because everyone else is. They become involved in the paranormal as a result of peer pressure. This is probably the number one reason for pollster George Barna's finding that 73 percent of America's youth have participated in psychic activities.[21]

A Feeling of Control

Certain teenagers are more likely than others to engage in dangerous spiritual experimentation—especially those who are relationally isolated and those who are experiencing significant stress and frustration.[22] Many such teens experiment with psychic activities and paranormal phenomena in order to control or influence their circumstances for the better. This gives them a false sense of control and a misguided sense of significance.

Latent Psychic Abilities

Psychics constantly disseminate the lie that every human being on earth has latent or hidden psychic powers. These paranormal abilities only need to be awakened and developed. Supposedly, because human beings utilize only 10 percent of their brains, their psychic powers are latent in the unused 90 percent.[23] Many people thus turn to psychics to learn from them how they too can become psychic.

James Van Praagh says a person's psychic sense is often referred to as a sixth sense, an intuition, a gut feeling, or a hunch. He says that all of us use this ability every day without even knowing it. He asks, "How many times have you thought of someone, and minutes later the phone rings and that person is on the other end of the line?"[24] That, he says, is an example of the sixth sense. In his book *Heaven and Earth,* he explains:

> We are born with six senses, not five. The sixth sense, the one most of us don't know how to apply in everyday life, is our intuition, inner voice, or psychic awareness. We all have this power, but for many people it remains repressed. Our sixth sense relies on our intellect, our five senses, and our emotions, and works in conjunction with any or all of them.[25]

Van Praagh also believes that all human beings have benevolent spirit guides. In his books, he provides readers with information and exercises that help them experience the presence of their spirit guides and learn from them. He is convinced that when a lightbulb flickers in a room, when a telephone rings and no one is there, and when a TV picture seems to scramble for no reason, a spirit guide may be seeking to make contact with you.[26]

Char Margolis is another popular psychic who believes all human beings have an innate psychic ability. "It's inherent in our makeup, in the same way we have sight, hearing, touch, taste, and smell."[27] She says part of her mission in life is to teach people how to recognize and act upon their psychic abilities. A proper use of the sixth sense, she says, will enrich one's life more than the other five senses combined. "Our intuitive sense is literally a channel between this world and the next. It's an energy conduit through which we can connect with loved ones who have died, speak to our guardian angels and spirit guides, and even touch the highest level of universal consciousness and love."[28] She encourages those who have doubts about themselves to become like the little engine that could: "I think I can, I think I can."[29]

The reasons for the current popularity of the paranormal are many and varied. The paranormal, of course, covers a broad range of phenomena, utilizing a vocabulary all its own. The next chapter will provide you with a primer on the paranormal. Think of it as a crash course in occultic terminology.

THREE

A PRIMER ON PSYCHIC PHENOMENA

A Primer on Psychic Phenomena
A Primer on Psychic Phenomena

H ave you ever visited a foreign country? If you have, you've probably known the feeling of not being able to speak someone else's language.

That's the way some people feel in discussions about psychics and the paranormal. Many of the words associated with this field of study seem foreign. This chapter is a user-friendly guide to such terms, an easy-to-use primer on the foreign language of psychic phenomena.

We will consider these terms under four broad headings:

• The Big Picture
• Contact with the Dead
• Psychic Tools of the Trade
• Ghost Phenomena

These categories will help you understand the terms. You'll see! (By the way, you can read and understand the rest of this book without trying to memorize the words in this chapter.)

The Big Picture

You will find four general terms scattered throughout this book: *occultism,* the *paranormal, divination,* and *psychic.* These terms are closely related. Understanding them provides an overview of psychic phenomena.

OCCULTISM

The word *occult* comes from the Latin word *occultus* and literally means "hidden," "secret," or "concealed." The term refers to hidden or secret knowledge, "to that which is beyond the range of ordinary human knowledge; to mysterious or concealed phenomena; to inexplicable events."[1] The term is frequently used in reference to certain practices or occult arts, including divination, contact with the dead (or *necromancy*), fortune-telling, and magic.

Occultism takes many forms, but often involves such practices as trance states, séances, clairvoyance, telepathy, psychometry, spiritism (also called *channeling*), automatic handwriting, peering into crystals, levitation, and out-of-body experiences.

THE PARANORMAL

Paranormal refers to that which goes above or beyond the normal, beyond what we can sense with our five senses. It can also refer to that which goes beyond scientific laws.

When people today speak of the paranormal, they are often speaking broadly of invisible forces, energies, powers, or spirits that cannot be objectively discerned or quantified. Some people use the term to refer to efforts to access or use supernatural power, or attempts to gain secret or hidden information outside the use of the natural senses.

DIVINATION

Divination (or *divining*) is an attempt to foresee or foretell future events, thereby discovering hidden or secret knowledge. The use of divination is nothing new; it existed even in Bible times. People of pagan nations often engaged in various forms of divination to determine the future or the will of the gods. Sometimes these ancient occultists would use spiritists or mediums to communicate with the dead or obtain paranormal information (Deuteronomy

18:11; 1 Samuel 28:3,9). Others used witchcraft to extract information from a pagan god (Numbers 22:7; 23:23; Joshua 13:22). Some in ancient times conjured spells (Deuteronomy 18:11) or practiced sorcery (Exodus 22:18; Deuteronomy 18:10). Others interpreted omens (Genesis 30:37; 44:5). Some in Babylon observed and interpreted the stars (astrology) because they believed the stars to be connected to the pagan gods (Daniel 1:20; 2:2,10,27; 4:7; 5:7,11,15). Still others practiced soothsaying by, for example, examining the liver of a dead animal that had been used for sacrifice. Abnormalities in the liver could indicate some aspect of the will of the gods.

Psychics continue to practice divination today. Popular forms of divination include astrology, peering into crystals, palm reading, fortune-telling, and contacting the dead (necromancy).

PSYCHIC

Psychic is a general term referring to a person who claims to be sensitive to phenomena beyond the five senses and who engages in one or more paranormal activities, including attempting to contact the dead, acting as a mouthpiece for spirit entities (including spirit guides and angels), and engaging in various forms of divination. Psychics claim to have various powers:

- *telepathy*—receiving or sending thoughts to another person
- *precognition*—supernatural knowledge of the future
- *clairvoyance*—seeing something beyond natural means about the past, present, or future

Some of today's prime-time psychics add further details regarding what they consider to be a psychic. James Van Praagh claims the spirit world vibrates at a faster frequency than ours. These spirits allegedly send communications faster than living people are used to. "It's as if we are communicating across a vast chasm without the help of a simultaneous translator." Psychic mediums, Van Praagh says, have the ability to discern these rapid-fire messages.[2]

John Edward compares psychic energy to radio waves. Even if

a person does not turn on the radio, the radio waves are still there. Turn on your radio, and you can pick up these invisible signals. When Edward does a psychic reading, he claims to metaphorically flick on his psychic switch and waits for the message to come through.[3]

Sylvia Browne claims different psychics have different abilities. "Just as a God-given musical gift can manifest itself in a variety of ways, from singer to composer to musician to conductor, the specifics of the psychic gift have varied from one generation of my family to another." She says that some in her family can go into a trance and allow a spirit entity to see, speak, and hear through them, while others in the family either can't or won't. Some in the family have psychokinetic power (the ability to manipulate tangible objects psychically), while others do not.[4] Psychics' alleged powers are varied.

Contact with the Dead

Let's narrow the field a bit and focus our attention on terms that relate specifically to contact with the dead—including *medium, channeler, spiritism, spirit guide, séance, automatic handwriting, electronic voice phenomena (EVP),* and *levitation.*

MEDIUM

A medium can supposedly reach through the veil between the spiritual and physical worlds, attune to the fast vibrations of the spirit world, and communicate messages from individual spirits on the Other Side to people on earth. The term *medium* suggests that the person is a go-between—that is, a mediator or middleman between the spiritual and physical worlds.[5]

Some psychic mediums, such as James Van Praagh, draw a distinction between *mental mediums* and *physical mediums*. A mental medium—the most common kind of medium—is one who makes use of his "intuitive mind." This intuitive mind is used for clairvoyance ("clear seeing" of the spirit world), clairaudience ("clear hearing" of the spirit world), or clairsentience ("clear feeling" of the spirit world).[6] (More on these "foreign words" below.)

The second type of medium is a physical medium. In contrast to a mental medium, in which only the mind of the medium is utilized, a physical medium makes his entire body available for a spirit entity.[7] Some of today's popular channelers, such as Kevin Ryerson, are physical mediums. (I've seen him do his stuff in person. Pretty weird!)

Van Praagh claims that every medium is a psychic, but not every psychic is a medium. What he means by this is that a person may possess psychic intuition without being able to attune to the alleged faster vibrational rate of the spirit world. Only a medium can interface between the high-speed spirit world and the low-speed physical world.[8] As psychic Sylvia Browne put it, "a medium is simply a person whose God-given psychic abilities are complemented by an expanded range of frequency perceptions. The result is that they're able to see, hear, and experience spirits from other dimensions who operate at higher frequency levels than ours on earth."[9] (Notice that Browne claims psychic abilities are "God-given." Later in the book, I'll demonstrate that God condemns all such activities.)

CHANNELER

A channeler is similar to a medium. Channeling is "the practice of attempting communication with departed human or extra-human intelligences (usually nonphysical) through the agency of a human medium, with the intent of receiving paranormal information."[10] Sylvia Browne tells us that "the communicating spirit never possesses, replaces, or eliminates the spirit of the channel [or channeler]. Instead, the channel simply withdraws or steps aside temporarily and acts as nothing more than a tube through which the communicating spirit can speak directly."[11]

Channelers sometimes do their work in a light trance and at other times in a deep trance. A deep trance includes an altered state of consciousness, making channelers entirely unaware of their surroundings. When they come out of the deep trance, they have no recollection of what has transpired. Channelers who do their work in a lighter trance are still aware of their surroundings and are still operating in a conscious, albeit altered, state.

Christian apologists John Ankerberg and John Weldon explain what typically occurs during a deep-trance channeling session:

> When a channeler goes into a full trance, it is as if he is falling backward into a deep sleep. Both his facial muscles and lips twitch as the invading spirit begins to gain control over the person. Once the spirit is in possession of the body, changes in breathing occur and the person's facial features and expressions are different, sometimes greatly different (for example, the late Jane Roberts). What can be most noticeable is when the voice changes; for example, a feminine voice becomes deep and masculine.[12]

Ankerberg and Weldon also note that during a deep-trance session, the channeler loses consciousness and does not remember what has taken place once the spirit entity has left the body. In these cases, the spirit so controls the deep-trance channeler that the channeler is much like a puppet being controlled by a greater power.[13]

Some channelers don't communicate with spirit entities. Instead, they claim to read the Akashic Records. The Akashic Records are allegedly an energy field that surrounds planet earth and psychically records all events in earth's history. Some psychics, such as Edgar Cayce and Levi Dowling, claim they can read the Akashic Records and provide secret information about the past.

SPIRITISM

Spiritism embraces the belief that the human personality continues to exist after death and that these personalities can be contacted in whatever spiritual plane or dimension they are in. *Spiritualism* is the proper name of the religion that involves contacting the dead. Spiritism and Spiritualism have often been popular during and after times of war. The living want to contact their dead loved ones who lost their lives during the war.

Psychic mediums claim these spirits actually desire contact with their living loved ones. Popular psychic Char Margolis explains:

> Death is almost always a difficult time for those of us who are left behind. But it is also the most common time for our loved ones to communicate with us from the Other Side. It's as if their spirits wanted to reassure us they are all right and still love us very much. These communications can come in the form of feelings, noises, strange experiences, "coincidences" that are too striking to be accidental, and so on.[14]

Christian scholar Kenneth Boa notes that the spiritist worldview recognizes escalating planes of existence. As spirits progressively evolve through higher and higher planes, communication with them allegedly becomes increasingly difficult.

> There are allegedly several planes of spiritual existence, and each spirit must progressively ascend to higher "heavens." As the spirit attains higher circles or spheres on the way to perfection, it gets less interested in the earthly sphere. Thus it becomes more difficult to communicate with the spirit as time goes on. Each new sphere is farther from the earth.[15]

One implication of this idea, occultists claim, is that the easiest time to communicate with dead loved ones is when they have recently died and have not yet evolved.

Spiritualism is perhaps the oldest religious cult in existence. Every known civilization has practiced it to one degree or another. Many ancient sources mention mediums, including the Bible and the literature of the Egyptians, Babylonians, Chinese, and Greeks.

The modern "Spiritualist movement" (involving spiritism) emerged in 1848 at the home of farmer John Fox in Hydesville, New York.[16] Fox's daughters—Margaret (1836–1893), Leah (1814–1890), and Catherine (1841–1892)—claimed to hear rapping sounds in the house and believed the sounds were a form of communication from the ghost of a murdered man by the name of Charles Rosma. The sisters became highly influential in the Spiritualist movement—at least up until 1886 when Margaret confessed that they were frauds. She claimed she produced the rappings by cracking her toe joints (she later retracted this confession). By this time, however, Spiritualism had established powerful momentum in American society. Margaret's confession was not enough to stop the momentum.

SPIRIT GUIDES

Modern psychics often claim that all people have spirit guides who can give them wisdom from the Other Side and assist them throughout life. Some psychics claim to be in conscious contact with their spirit guides. Others say that their spirit guides typically manifest themselves through a hunch or a subtle feeling that comes over them.[17]

Most psychics believe spirit guides are tied to the process of reincarnation. The idea is that when people die, they go to the Other Side, where they commune with other spirits. After an indeterminate time—10 years, 100 years, 500 years, or whatever—each spirit allegedly incarnates into another human body.

Before incarnating into another body, the person allegedly asks someone he or she trusts on the Other Side to be his or her spirit guide. Sylvia Browne claims that "every one of us has a Spirit Guide, someone we literally trusted with our soul on the Other Side, who agreed to be our constant, vigilant companion and helpmate when we made the choice to experience another lifetime on earth."[18] This guide might be a mother or father, a grandparent, an aunt or uncle, or perhaps a friend. Browne claims that because spirit guides have experienced at least one incarnation on earth, they are able to empathize with common problems, mistakes, temptations, fears, and frailties. Everyone, Browne says, gets to be someone else's spirit guide at some point or another.

Van Praagh adds that before people on the Other Side decide to incarnate into another human body, they map out a blueprint for their life's journey, clearly delineating the lessons they want to learn during this lifetime. Once they are incarnated, should they veer off the chosen path, their spirit guides seek to get them back on track so they are again in line with their blueprint.[19]

SÉANCE

A séance is a meeting of people who attempt to communicate with the spirit world or with souls of departed people through a medium. In most cases, people try to contact recently departed people during the séance. Mediums often use the assistance of a spirit guide, a Ouija board, and/or automatic handwriting (see below).

During a séance, everyone holds hands, the medium goes into a trance, and a spirit or spirit guide allegedly takes control of the medium and speaks through his or her voice. In some séances, the medium brings a musical instrument, and the spirit may purportedly play the instrument. In some cases, the spirit will allegedly communicate by guiding the medium's handwriting. Sometimes objects in the room allegedly move. A spirit entity may even appear in a mist-like form known as *ectoplasm* (see below).[20]

AUTOMATIC HANDWRITING

Automatic handwriting is a phenomenon in Spiritualism in which a medium allegedly writes words without apparent awareness. A dead person's spirit or a paranormal entity supposedly controls the medium's hand. During the writing, the medium is typically unaware of the information being communicated.

An example of automatic handwriting is the book *A Course in Miracles,* written by Helen Schucman, as guided by a spirit entity named Jesus. This spirit guided Schucman's hand in all that she wrote in this three-volume tome.

ELECTRONIC VOICE PHENOMENA (EVP)

Occultists believe that spirits can communicate with the living in clever ways. They can allegedly manipulate static on radios, imprint images on television sets, and even impress voices upon magnetic tape. This is known as electronic voice phenomena (EVP).[21] *White Noise* is a recent movie that popularized this phenomenon.

LEVITATION

Levitation comes from a Latin word meaning "to ease" or "to lift" and refers to the alleged phenomenon of "free floating," in which an animate or inanimate object is reportedly suspended in the air with no apparent means of support. In some séances, the Spiritualist's table reportedly lifts off the ground, allegedly indicating the presence of spirit beings or paranormal entities.

Psychic Tools of the Trade

Psychics and mediums utilize what one might call psychic "tools of the trade," including the trance state, clairvoyance, clairaudience, clairsentience, psychometry, crystal balls, aura reading, and out-of-body experiences.

TRANCE STATE

A trance state is an altered state of consciousness, a mental state other than normal waking consciousness, that ranges from a mild sense of the transcendent to a deep trance. People report that trances often bring a sense of oneness with all things and a sense of harmony with the universe. This state is sometimes referred to as *cosmic consciousness*. Trances enable mediums to have mystical experiences with spiritual entities.

CLAIRVOYANCE

Clairvoyance—literally, "clear vision"—is the alleged mental "seeing" of physical objects or events at a distance by psychic means. It also involves the alleged ability to perceive things beyond physical reality, things in the ethereal dimension, the realm of spirits. This perception usually involves a flash of insight. Clairvoyance may include the alleged psychic ability to see and describe future events. Psychics sometimes claim to use clairvoyance when helping the police solve crimes. Sylvia Browne claims to have helped police solve dozens of crimes. Browne says, "Clairvoyants have what's sometimes called 'second sight,' which allows their eyes to perceive a wider range of input and frequencies than normal."[22]

CLAIRAUDIENCE

Clairaudience—literally, "clear hearing"—involves hearing with the psychic ear or the sensitized ear. A clairaudient claims to be "able to hear sounds, names, voices, and music that vibrate on a higher frequency."[23] Just as dogs have the capability to hear a higher frequency than humans, mediums claim to hear beyond the normal hearing range into the world of spirits.

CLAIRSENTIENCE

Clairsentience—literally, "clear feeling"—involves allegedly receiving a projected emotion from nearby or from another (spiritual) dimension and experiencing that emotional sensation personally.[24] "A true clairsentient will usually feel the spirit personality coming through his entire being."[25]

PSYCHOMETRY

Psychometry is the alleged ability to psychically sense the history of an object, such as a brush or a photograph. The psychic goes into a trance, holds the object, and then seeks to interpret the alleged emanations of energy that come from the object. By using psychometry, the psychic claims he can sense who owns the object and whether the owner is living or has crossed over to the Other Side.

CRYSTAL BALLS

Some fortune-tellers seek paranormal information or knowledge of the future by peering into crystals (or a crystal ball). "Gazing into the glass, the clairvoyant enters into a trance-like state and is able to view future events."[26]

Many people have the mistaken notion that as the psychic gazes into the crystal ball, he or she sees something in the ball itself. In reality, the crystal ball merely enables the medium to focus. Gazing into it brings images or words to the medium's mind. The gazing itself may help induce an altered state of consciousness, which subsequently brings about a psychic vision.

AURA READING

Occultists believe an aura is an invisible energy—a "life force"—that emanates from within a person and surrounds the physical body. Parapsychologist Hazel Denning explains:

> In a healthy body the aura extends out from the body in thread-like emanations. Illness in the body is indicated by a drooping aura. The basic aura is white and extends out from the body about an inch or two.[27]

Mediums claim to be able to read auras. They say they can derive information about a person's personality, needs, and even illnesses by noting variations in the hue of his or her aura. A shriveled aura indicates impending death.[28]

OUT-OF-BODY EXPERIENCES

In an out-of-body experience, also called *astral projection*, the body remains stationary while one's soul or spirit allegedly leaves the body and travels to different locations in the blink of an eye. The soul can allegedly travel nearby (say, to a neighbor's house) or unlimited distances into outer space. As one psychic put it, "Astral travel is nothing more than our spirits taking a break from these cumbersome, gravity-challenged bodies they're housed in and taking off to visit whomever or wherever we want."[29]

Some psychics claim that during their out-of-body experiences, they commune with and learn from spiritually advanced persons. Some are so bold as to claim that their astral travels have penetrated to the very sphere of God.

Occultists often speak of a thin gray cord that remains connected between one's soul and the body at the navel. Should this cord be broken, the body dies and the soul crosses over to the Other Side.

Shirley MacLaine has claimed to experience this phenomenon.

Ghost Phenomena

This final category includes terms related to ghost phenomena, including *poltergeists, materialization, transfiguration, apport,* and *spirit photography.* You'll see that these terms are easy to understand.

GHOSTS

A ghost is allegedly a noncorporeal (nonmaterial) phantomlike manifestation of a dead person or animal. It is supposedly the spirit, soul, specter, or "astral body" of a person (or animal) who has not yet entered the Other Side but instead has remained on earth after death. Sometimes the ghost is semitransparent, shadowy, or foggy. Parapsychologists often call this fog-like substance *ectoplasm.* Sometimes ghosts do not manifest themselves visibly but allegedly move objects, make noise (like footsteps), or flip on light switches.[30]

Sylvia Browne claims that the majority of spirits proceed through a tunnel into white light (the Other Side) following the moment of death. Some, however, refuse to enter the tunnel and choose instead to remain on earth, without their bodies, hanging around for a variety of reasons.[31] I will discuss ghosts in greater detail in chapter 4, "Alleged Ghosts and Hauntings." Then, chapter 5, "The Truth About Ghosts and Hauntings," will demonstrate that ghost and poltergeist phenomena involve not the spirits of dead humans but rather demonic spirits.

POLTERGEISTS

Polter is the German word for "noisy" or "rumbling." *Geist* is the German word for "ghost" or "spirit." *Poltergeist* therefore refers to a noisy ghost or noisy spirit. A poltergeist is supposedly an intrusive invisible prankster ghost that is noisy (ringing bells, for example) and disruptive, and that moves inanimate objects, like furniture. Foul smells, cold rooms, and apparitions may allegedly be associated with this phenomenon.[32] Such poltergeists may be either benevolent or malevolent.

James Van Praagh suggests that "poltergeists can be attributed to earthbound spirits that are trying to get the attention of the living."[33] Poltergeist phenomena are generally confined to a single house. Van Praagh believes that "many spirits on the other side are involved in rescuing these lost and misguided souls."[34]

MATERIALIZATION

A materialization is a rare phenomenon in which a ghost or spirit allegedly takes shape using ectoplasm. As Van Praagh describes it, "A gauzelike, colorless and odorless substance known as ectoplasm will emerge from the ears, nose, mouth, or solar plexus area of the medium and form into 'physical' matter." Either a part of the spirit (partial limbs, face, head, or torso) or the entire spirit may take shape using this substance.[35] According to some, the spirits of animals can also materialize.[36]

TRANSFIGURATION

A spirit from the Other Side can allegedly impose its own face on the face of a medium. This phenomenon is known as transfiguration. For example, a young female medium could take on the facial appearance of an old man. Animal spirits can also allegedly appear through transfiguration.[37]

APPORT

The word *apport*, from the Latin word *apportare*, refers to objects that allegedly appear out of thin air in a room, usually during a séance.[38] They are typically small objects, such as jewels, stones, coins, or flowers.[39]

SPIRIT PHOTOGRAPHY

According to psychics, cameras are far more sensitive to light waves than the human eye, so they can detect and record things we cannot see. Psychics claim cameras can detect the energy bodies of spirits that are invisible to the human eye.[40] Weekend psychic fairs often offer courses on spirit photography.

That wasn't so bad, was it? It's all pretty weird, though!

Having finished this brief crash course on occultic terminology, we will now take a more in-depth look at alleged ghosts and hauntings. Be prepared for some more strange claims!

FOUR

ALLEGED GHOSTS AND HAUNTINGS

W hile doing research for this book, I ordered a bunch of
the most popular ghost books from the Barnes and Noble
online store, where I've ordered hundreds of books in the past.
Several weeks after I placed the order, I received a phone call from
their customer service department. The representative told me
that while the box of books had been en route to me, it had been
obliterated, and not a single book could be found anywhere. I said,
"Okay..." My eyes narrowed. The person on the phone said she
would immediately put together another shipment of the same
books and rush them out to me. I said, "That's fine."

After I hung up the phone, I wondered to myself, *Are the powers
of darkness trying to hinder my research? Maybe the devil doesn't
want me to see those books.* But then I thought, *"Hmm...perhaps
God doesn't want me to see those books.* That seemed an unlikely
scenario to me, however, because as a professional apologist I've
been reading cultic and occultic books for decades. Then I thought
to myself, *Well, ya know, it could just be bad postal service!*

In any event, the books finally arrived, and after reading them,
I have to say that a lot of people have given considerable thought
to ghosts in modern times. In fact, 38 percent of Americans believe

not only that ghosts exist but also that they can come back and visit us. That's well over a third of all Americans.

In this chapter, we'll look at some of the most common ideas about ghosts that are presently circulating in America. Then, in chapter 5, I will offer a critique of these ideas.

What Is a Ghost?

A ghost, according to psychics, is a nonmaterial phantomlike manifestation of a dead person—or, in some cases, of an animal. It is supposedly the spirit, soul, specter, or "astral body" of a person (or animal) who has not passed over to the Other Side but instead has remained on earth after death. Psychic Sylvia Browne claims that at death, the spirits of most people accept the reality of their deaths and immediately go through some kind of tunnel to enter into the spirit dimension known as the *Other Side*.[1] On the Other Side, these spirits can allegedly continue to progress and evolve. A ghost, however, either "sees the tunnel and turns away or refuses to acknowledge the tunnel in the first place, with the result that it gets caught, outside of its body, between our dimension and the dimension of the Other Side."[2]

Psychics claim that when these ghost spirits don't enter the tunnel that leads to the Other Side, they exist under the confusing delusion that they are still alive and have not died. Paranormal investigator Leslie Rule claims that such ghosts "have no sense of passing time. A century may be just seconds on the Other Side. Trapped souls seem to exist in a state of confusion. It may feel a little like being stuck in a dream."[3]

Psychics claim that such ghosts recognize that, for some reason, the world seems to treat them as if they no longer exist. This can allegedly add to the ghost's confusion.[4] A situation similar to this was portrayed by Bruce Willis in the motion picture, *The Sixth Sense*. Willis's character had been killed, and his spirit stayed on earth, not realizing he was dead until the end of the movie.

Browne claims that once a spirit actually enters into the Other Side, psychics cannot easily see or hear them because they exist in an entirely different spirit dimension. However, ghosts have not yet entered that dimension, so they are allegedly easier to see and hear.[5] "Because they are stubbornly clinging to this dimension after death, they are the easiest residents of the spirit world for the rest of us to hear and see."[6]

When such ghosts appear, they are supposedly semitransparent, shadowy, and fog-like. Parapsychologists call this fog-like substance *ectoplasm*. Sometimes ghosts do not actually manifest themselves visibly but allegedly make their presence known by moving objects, making noise (such as footsteps), or flipping on a light switch.[7]

Why Ghosts Allegedly Come Back

Why do ghosts choose not to enter into the tunnel so they can live on the Other Side? Psychics offer a variety of opinions on this issue. Char Margolis, for example, suggests they refuse to enter the tunnel because they simply do not wish to progress. She claims they are often attached to a place or a living person on earth. "These people still love you, still want to comfort you. Love does not die because a person has died. The connection has been there, and always will be."[8] Parapsychologist Hazel Denning claims that "the spirit…is often greatly distressed by the anguish it observes in the loved one in mourning. With genuine love, the spirit reaches out to assure the grieving relative or friend of its well being."[9]

Psychics sometimes claim that ghosts hang around on the earth because their living loved ones do not want them to go. Margolis says, "I've known individuals who refuse to let the spirit of their departed spouses go, even though the spirit truly wants to progress to the next level."[10] She thus claims that one of the best gifts we can give our dead loved ones is the permission for them to move on to the Other Side, where they can continue to progress.

James Van Praagh claims that some ghosts hang around on earth and return to their old surroundings if they left earth suddenly or violently (for example, if they died in a violent car accident). Because of the suddenness of their death, Van Praagh claims, they may not be fully aware of what has happened to them. That's why they may think they're still alive.

Van Praagh claims other ghosts may return to protect or warn a loved one of being in danger.[11] This was portrayed in the movie *Ghost* when the ghost character played by Patrick Swayze tried to warn his still-living girlfriend that she was in physical danger.[12]

Van Praagh also claims ghosts may return to take care of unfinished business. For example, if a person was murdered, he may return as a ghost to seek justice or revenge. This too was illustrated in the movie *Ghost*, with the ghost character played by Patrick Swayze seeking justice for his killers.[13] Once justice is obtained, psychics claim, ghosts feel free to move on to the Other Side.

Yet another possibility, Van Praagh claims, is that if a criminal dies, his or her ghost may seek to remain on the earth plane in order to avoid having to go to hell or purgatory. In this case, the ghost is acting out of a sense of self-preservation.[14]

Other psychics claim ghosts may hang around on earth just because they're curious about what's going on down here. "It's just to see what is going on in the world of the living; they come back to check on everybody...They're curious, just as they were in life."[15]

Or, psychics say, ghosts may hang around on earth because of personal greed. "A preoccupation with land or money has at times been carried to the beyond. There are many reports of possessive beings who cannot seem to let go of their earthly valuables."[16]

Finally, some psychics claim, a ghost may return if the person who died did not receive a proper burial or if his or her grave has been desecrated in some way.[17] This is illustrated in the blockbuster movie *Poltergeist*, where a housing development was built on top of an old graveyard that had been relocated to another part of town.

Alleged Indications of a Ghost

Psychics claim a number of signs can indicate a ghost may be present. Auditory signs include footsteps, rapping noises in a wall, ringing bells (like a telephone), disembodied laughter and screams, or a whisper. Objects may be displaced. Pets may engage in strange behavior, such as a dog barking at thin air.

Psychics often claim that if a ghost is present, the room might suddenly become cold, as portrayed in the movie *The Sixth Sense*. A sudden breeze might fill the room. One might encounter strange smells—pervasive fragrances or even vile stenches.[18] Psychics claim lights might turn on and off at random or just flicker rapidly, toilets might flush at random, and electrical appliances might turn on and off at random.[19] Sometimes a ghost will allegedly burn out a light-bulb—but only when a living person is around to witness it.[20]

In some cases, psychics say, people may have the strange feeling that someone is present or that they are being watched—a feeling that makes the hair rise on the back of the neck (as in *The Sixth Sense*).[21] People might feel a tap on the shoulder or sense someone brushing past them. Doors or cabinets might open, seemingly by themselves.[22]

Psychics also report instances of electronic voice phenomena. A face of a dead loved one might appear in the white noise of a TV set not tuned to a particular channel, or a voice might speak in the white noise of a radio not tuned to a particular channel.[23]

Psychics also report sightings of visible but transparent, fog-like apparitions. In some cases, one might just see a shadow. Paranormal investigators say that such appearances can happen in various places. For example, a ghost figure may be peering out a window. People outside the house are usually the ones who claim to see a figure peering out. Other times a ghost may allegedly appear in the reflection of a mirror, perhaps peering over your shoulder (as in Reese Witherspoon's movie, *Just Like Heaven*). In other cases, the ghost may be on a staircase, or perhaps in a hallway.[24] In some cases, a ghost may allegedly have inappropriate clothing on, such as wearing an overcoat in the middle of summer.

Paranormal investigators claim that such phenomena may take place so fast that a person may wonder whether they actually occurred at all. "Often just one person witnesses this type of paranormal event that is over so swiftly it is as if the universe hiccuped. Things were out of kilter for a fraction of a moment. The next moment, everything was normal again."[25] People often wonder, *Did that really just happen?*

Alleged Poltergeist Activity

As we've seen, a *poltergeist* is a "noisy ghost" or "noisy spirit."[26] It is a noisy and disruptive intruder.[27] Psychics claim these spirits like to pull pranks on people—such as bucking beds and throwing items around in the house.[28] A sensationalized portrayal of this is in Steven Spielberg's *Poltergeist*, where one of the children's rooms is so infested by poltergeists that virtually dozens of items fly around the room.

Alleged Hauntings

People are fascinated by the phenomena of haunted houses, hotels, and other sites. Popular books on the subject include *Coast to Coast Ghosts: True Stories of Hauntings Across America, Haunted Houses: Chilling Tales from 24 American Homes,* and *Hauntings: Real-Life Encounters with Troubled Spirits.* In this genre, the Travel Channel features *America's Most Haunted Places* and *Haunted Hotels.* Court TV likewise features a show called *Haunting Evidence.* For whatever reason, millions of Americans believe that hauntings are genuinely taking place in our midst.

Hauntings occur when earthbound spirits allegedly choose to stay behind on earth instead of entering the "perfect joy" of the Other Side. The spirits then choose to reveal themselves by various means to the new occupants of their former habitation.[29] Sylvia Browne assures us that hauntings are much more common than most of us think! I'll provide two representative examples of claims of modern hauntings.

A RUDE AWAKENING IN THE NIGHT

Parapsychologist Hazel Denning, in her book *Hauntings: Real-Life Encounters with Troubled Spirits,* describes a lady who allegedly encountered a nighttime haunting. Her husband was away at a banker's convention, so she was alone with their baby son for a week. One night, she awoke at 3:00 AM and sensed she was not alone. She first suspected a burglar might be in the house, and she very cautiously opened her eyes. The street lamps outside illuminated her room well enough, but she saw nothing unusual. She turned her head slowly to take in the entire room. She saw nothing but still had the heavy feeling of a presence nearby. Goose bumps erupted on her arms. Panic, terror, and helplessness pressed in on her, and she pulled the covers up over her head. Nothing happened. She eventually calmed down enough to fall back asleep.

The woman had a similar experience a few nights later while her husband was still away. She recalls, "I sat bolt upright in bed. In as firm a voice as I could manage I said, 'This is MY house, you have no right to be here, so get…OUT, NOW, and don't come back.'"[30] The lady claims the atmosphere in her house changed dramatically and the oppressive feeling lifted. She believes she experienced a haunting, though it ceased after her confrontation of the unwelcome spirit.

A TERRIFIED SON

The book *I Never Believed in Ghosts Until…* recounts an alleged haunting of a boy's room. The mother claims she used to get peeved at her son Ed because when she went to his room to awaken him for school or work, he was never there. She would usually find him sleeping on the couch in the den. She later discovered the reason he would never sleep in his own room: He was terrified in there. He claims he had been awakened on numerous occasions, usually in the early morning hours, with the sensation that someone was in the room even though he couldn't see anyone. During these times he would feel paralyzed, unable to move a finger, for what seemed like the longest time. He claims that on several occasions he awoke only to find himself being dropped onto the bed. He never saw anything. He just had the sensation of a presence in the room. The only time he could get a good night's sleep was when he slept in the den.[31]

Paranormal Investigation Teams

Because of the preponderance of alleged hauntings around the country, paranormal investigation teams seem to be springing up everywhere. Such groups often use a battery of high-tech equipment in their investigations. For example, they'll use electromagnetic field meters because ghosts allegedly give out a much lower magnetic reading than man-made objects in the home. They take temperature readings because ghosts allegedly bring a sudden drop in temperature. Sometimes they use thermal cameras, which reveal cold spots in the room, allegedly indicating the location of spirits.[32] They also do audio recordings because the naked ear might not pick up everything that is going on in a room or house.[33]

One such paranormal research group is the Southern Wisconsin Paranormal Research Group. They do not make use of psychics, séances, or Ouija boards, nor are they ghost busters. Rather, "the team uses high-tech hardware to investigate and document paranormal activity throughout the Midwest, to bring credibility to parapsychology."[34]

The founder of this group says that 98 percent of what the Paranormal Research Group finds is normal and natural. "I think a lot of people come into it thinking, 'I'm going to see ghosts.' Well, that just doesn't happen."[35]

When the group goes into the field and does an investigation, they take along an armory of recording equipment and sensitive electronic devices designed to measure the electromagnetic spectrum. They also use digital and conventional cameras, as well as a tape recorder to capture electronic voice phenomena.[36]

Another such group is the Little Egypt Paranormal Investigation Team in Vienna, Illinois. The founder of the group was a skeptic about ghost appearances until her three-year-old son matter-of-factly announced that he had just seen his grandparents in his room (both had died recently). She wanted to find out what was going on, so she founded a paranormal investigation team. When she investigates an alleged haunting, she first does a daytime walk-through to get a feel for the layout of the place and to get a sense of what is normal. Next she will visit the location at dusk and begin looking for ghosts. "We'll talk to the spirits," she said. "We'll tell them we are trying to find proof they are there. I think they want us to know they are there." So far, she has not seen any ghosts.[37]

Taking Your House Back

Psychics and paranormal investigators claim that if your house is haunted and ghosts are bothering you, you can take your house back! Different psychics suggest different solutions.

One psychic claims you need to "talk to them. You demand they go to one room of the house or to the attic."[38] That way, only *part* of your house is haunted. The rest of the house is clean of ghost activity.

Van Praagh claims one can cleanse a house by meditating. During such meditation, a person sends thoughts to the troubled spirit. When sending thoughts to the ghost, Van Praagh says, encourage it to ask for a parent or grandparent spirit to guide it into the Other Side. Then encourage it by letting it know it will be much happier on the Other Side. Cleansing the house in this way, Van Praagh says, may take from a few days to a few weeks.[39]

Parapsychologist Loyd Auerbach has come up with some rather novel ways of getting rid of ghosts. He claims to annoy them by playing obnoxious music accompanied by strange light effects. (If this were effective, one would naturally expect that ghosts would never haunt houses where teenagers live!) Or, Auerbach says, you can get a book of corny knock-knock jokes, read them aloud, and inform the ghost that this will continue until it leaves. The ghost will allegedly leave soon enough![40]

Paranormal investigator Nancy Myer suggests do's and don'ts when cleansing one's house of ghosts. Don't use occultic paraphernalia such as Ouija boards or tarot cards. Don't engage in occultic practices such as séances. These things will only make hauntings worse, Myer claims.

On the other hand, do visualize your house being permeated

with emerald-green light. Follow this by visualizing white light energy flooding your house. These are allegedly strong positive energies. Negative energies, such as naughty ghosts, have trouble staying in a place loaded up with green and white light. This visualization technique may take several weeks to cleanse your house.[41]

All Ghosts Eventually Go into the Light

Regardless of which technique one uses to cleanse one's house, psychics claim that all ghosts eventually find their way into the light on the Other Side. The biggest hurdle, Sylvia Browne says, is convincing these spirits that they're dead. Once they are convinced, talking them into moving on is easier.[42] Fortunately, Browne says, spirits on the Other Side are allegedly aware of these troubled spirits and are involved in their own compassionate interventions so that they'll all finally make it into the light on the Other Side.[43]

FIVE

THE TRUTH ABOUT GHOSTS AND HAUNTINGS

Many today are convinced by the evidence for ghostly phenomena—that is, they believe *dead human beings* make appearances among us. Many books provide evidence for these appearances. However, we need to remember something that Solomon—the wisest man who ever lived (1 Kings 3:12; 4:29-32; 5:12; 10:23)—said on one occasion: "The first to present his case seems right, till another comes forward and questions him" (Proverbs 18:17). The case for dead humans appearing among us may seem strong to some until further evidence pokes holes in the theory.

Many verses in Scripture encourage Christians to exercise wisdom and discernment so that we will not be deceived:

- Proverbs 3:21 exhorts, "My son, preserve sound judgment and discernment, do not let them out of your sight."
- Ephesians 4:14 urges us to "no longer be infants, tossed back and forth by the waves, and blown here and there by every wind of teaching and by the cunning and craftiness of men in their deceitful scheming." In other words, don't believe everything you hear!
- First Timothy 4:7 warns, "Have nothing to do with godless myths and old wives' tales."

• Zechariah 8:16 instructs us to "speak the truth to each other."

My goal in this chapter is to speak the truth. Let's resolve to take some initial steps toward dispelling myths and focus on sound judgment and discernment.

Ghost Phenomena Is Experience-Based

One cannot help but note that much of the so-called evidence for ghost phenomena is based on experience and feelings, not objective data. One ghost enthusiast commented on "feeling like you are being watched and you don't see anyone there," and makes reference to "goose-bumps, hair standing on the back of our neck, and a feeling of cold." This enthusiast reported, "Lots of times I would like to say 'oh yeah, that is just the wind, I am just imagining it,' but you just have to experience it."[1] With all due respect, if one is going to make extraordinary claims, one must back up those claims with extraordinary evidence, not mere feelings.

Peripheral vision is very sensitive to motion. The problem is that peripheral vision does not focus on specific shapes. It simply detects motion. Some people, when they sense a random motion outside of their focused view, jump to the conclusion that a ghost just went by.[2] In reality, a passing car may have caused a brief reflection of light to shine into the house. Experiences can be deceiving. They are highly subjective and can easily be misinterpreted.

Another problem is that people may not necessarily report their experiences accurately. As one analyst said, trusting someone's experience "is fine so long as one can be certain that the experience they had was exactly the same as the one they reported. I doubt the match is usually this exact."[3] The lack of reliable reporting is well illustrated in the alleged crash of a UFO at Roswell, New Mexico. A *U.S. News & World Report* article gives this report:

> Many of Roswell's key witnesses have changed their story several times and have been caught telling falsehoods...A first group of eyewitnesses mistakenly believed

that some debris from a shattered radar reflector came from a spaceship. These witnesses didn't say anything about alien bodies. After a 1989 TV episode of *Unsolved Mysteries* about Roswell, a second mélange of "witnesses" came forward with bizarre tales of alien sightings. No one in this second group has told a plausible or consistent story. Jim Ragsdale, for one, said he spotted four alien bodies near a spaceship. Later he asserted that he saw nine alien bodies, in which he removed gold helmets, and that he buried the aliens in the sand.[4]

This episode illustrates the all-too-common tendency for people to embellish what they have experienced, often adding sensational details to make their stories seem more interesting and fascinating. This tendency keeps us from trusting many of the accounts people have given through the years of alleged encounters with ghosts.

Sleep and Ghost Phenomena

A key factor undermining at least some reports of ghost activity is that they often involve a person coming out of a deep sleep. One individual claimed to have woken in the middle of the night and said he saw someone in his bedroom, and then in his closet, and then standing next to his dresser. He said his wife was sound asleep, so the alleged apparition could not be confirmed.

When a person wakes up from sleep, his cognitive and perceptual abilities may be weak, and he may think he is experiencing something which in fact is not real.[5] A person can wake from a dream and think he still hears voices in the house. Once the person is completely awake, such strange experiences vanish.

Some people might have a night fear and wrongly attribute it to ghostly or paranormal phenomena. A night fear is an intense fear of something that poses no actual danger. During a night fear, people can experience a variety of symptoms, including shortness of breath, rapid breathing, irregular heartbeat, sweating, nausea, a sense of detachment from reality, and overall feelings of dread.

Some people, in such a state, may wrongly interpret their experience as a ghost haunting their house.

Misinterpretations Are All Too Easy

Some people have claimed house hauntings when in reality they have probably just misinterpreted the data. For example, one person was sure her house had been invaded by ghosts when she saw one of her paintings hanging higher than she thought it previously had. She also noted a large tablecloth on the kitchen table hanging nearly off the table onto the floor when she arrived home from work, but the flowers, phone book, and other items on the table had not moved. She further claims that food had vanished from her refrigerator.

This hardly constitutes proof for ghostly activity. Many explanations for what occurred in this woman's house are possible. The woman herself could have hung the painting higher and later forgot she had done so. She may have somehow misadjusted the tablecloth on the kitchen table without realizing it. She may have simply forgotten that she had eaten certain items in her refrigerator. A mischievous teenager could be involved. Who knows? Whatever the explanation, though, we see no compelling reason to suspect any kind of paranormal intrusion.[6]

Extraordinary claims call for extraordinary evidence. This ought to be a working policy for all those who suspect ghost phenomena.

The Power of Suggestion and Conditioning

An interesting psychological phenomenon is that people tend to see what they have been conditioned to see. For example, at the height of the European witch craze of the fifteenth and sixteenth centuries—in which people had become *programmed* to see witches—virtually thousands of people reported seeing flying witches. "I wouldn't have *seen* it if I hadn't *believed* it" seems to be a fitting twist on an old maxim.

In like manner, because of the many popular movies, television shows, and books about ghostly phenomena, some people have become programmed to expect the paranormal. One critic has noticed a "significant correlation between media depictions of paranormal events and peoples' views of paranormal claims... Media depictions of the paranormal do seem to influence the way people think about the subject."[7]

Fraudulent Claims

Let's be honest. Just as some of today's psychics engage in fraudulent activity (I'll document this later in the book), so do some who claim to see ghosts. I showed a professional photographer some of the ghost photographs I've come across, and I asked him what he thought. More specifically, I was interested in whether such photos could easily be produced without any real ghosts involved. He looked at the photos, grinned, and said it would be a piece of cake. He confirmed what I suspected all along—that someone who knows what he or she is doing with a camera can take some great ghost photos—without any ghosts involved at all.

Ghosts and the Occult

One might get the idea that I dismiss *all* alleged paranormal encounters as either fraudulent, a misinterpretation of the data, sheer subjectivism ("I feel like I'm being watched"), or the result of awakening from deep sleep. This is not the case.

Though alleged ghost encounters can be explained in this way, people sometimes genuinely encounter a spirit entity—*though not a dead human*. Some people encounter *demonic* spirits who may mimic dead people in order to deceive the living (see 1 John 4:1; 1 Timothy 4:1-3). Many who claim to have encountered such spirit entities have some prior involvement in the occult.

A growing corpus of evidence suggests that poltergeist phenomena are directly related to demonism and not to dead humans. People who are involved in some form of the occult—such as spiritism, necromancy, and séances—are often the ones who experience such poltergeist phenomena. John Ankerberg and John Weldon thus conclude that "the poltergeist phenomenon and its occult connection offer strong empirical evidence for the demonic nature of the spirits. In fact, we know of no poltergeist case that cannot be accounted for on the basis of this theory."[8]

In cases that do not involve fraudulence, mere experientialism, or awakening from deep sleep, a demonic spirit may indeed be causing paranormal phenomena. When I come across such a case, the first thing I want to know is, has the relevant person ever been involved in any form of the occult? Has he or she played with a Ouija board, participated in a séance, or consulted with a psychic to contact the dead? Such involvement is likely because of the strong occult-demon connection.

The Dangers of Occultism

This calls for a very strong warning. The person who dabbles in occultism—whether consulting a psychic, playing with a Ouija board, participating in a séance, or engaging in other forms of divination—might experience more severe consequences than just poltergeist phenomena. Experts who have studied such phenomena report that those who dabble in the occult might experience compulsive thoughts, anxiety, destructive tendencies, a tendency toward violence, mental illness, psychoses, fatal accidents, suicide, blasphemous thoughts, an aversion to God's Word and to prayer, instability, nervousness, severe depression, and even insanity.[9]

Amazingly, even psychics themselves warn against some of the "evil energies" one might encounter in participating in certain occultic practices. Char Margolis, for example, claims "there are energies and spirits out there that do not wish us well and want to trick us…In some ways, I believe using psychic tools like Ouija boards can be as dangerous for kids as taking drugs."[10] Psychic Nancy Myer agrees, noting that the Ouija board "opens a portal to the other side that is almost impossible to close." Understandably, she urges all people to avoid the Ouija. Dale Kaczmarek, a paranormal investigator, also agrees, warning that "many violent, negative, and potentially dangerous conditions are present to those using the board."[11] My point, of course, is that if psychics themselves warn us about encountering evil spiritual entities during occultic practices, then these evil entities must truly be evil indeed!

Of course, I must warn of a further deception. When psychics speak about the danger of certain occultic practices, they imply that consulting *with them* to contact the dead is safe. Let us be clear: Consulting with a psychic like Char Margolis or Nancy Myer can open you up to demonic affliction just as easily as playing with a Ouija board. Scripture therefore condemns *all* forms of occultism (Deuteronomy 18:9-13). Reader beware!

Dead Humans Are Not Ghosts

Another reason we know that genuine encounters with spirits involve demons and not dead humans is this: The Bible indicates that dead humans are not even available for earth visits as ghosts. At death, the believer's spirit departs from the physical body and immediately goes into the presence of the Lord in heaven (Philippians 1:21-23). This is why, when Stephen was being put to death by stoning, he prayed, "Lord Jesus, receive my spirit" (Acts 7:59). At the moment of death "the spirit returns to God who gave it" (Ecclesiastes 12:7).

In 2 Corinthians 5:8 we learn that Christians who are "away from the body" are "at home with the Lord." The Greek word *pros* is used for "with" in the phrase "at home with the Lord." This word suggests very close, face-to-face fellowship. It is a word used of intimate relationships. The verse thereby indicates that the fellowship we will have with Christ immediately following physical death will be very intimate. Don't miss this point: *Christians who have died are not still on earth but are with the Lord in heaven, where they remain in intimate perpetual fellowship with Him.*

For the unbeliever, death holds grim prospects. At death the unbeliever's spirit does not go to heaven but is involuntarily confined to a place of great suffering (Luke 16:19-31). Second Peter 2:9

tells us that the Lord knows how "to hold the unrighteous for the day of judgment, while continuing their punishment." *The unrighteous are not still on earth, nor do they have access to earth!*

Whatever people are encountering at alleged haunted houses and hotels is most certainly *not* the spirits of dead people walking around. As I have shown, the biblical evidence suggests that if a person is encountering any spirit entity at all (for example, through occult practices), it is a demonic spirit.

The Great Masquerade

Scripture supports the idea that Satan and his horde of demons have the ability to impersonate dead humans. They do so in order to give credence to the false religion of Spiritualism and lead millions of people astray. We must not forget that Satan is a masterful counterfeiter.

- Satan has his own church—the "synagogue of Satan" (Revelation 2:9).
- Satan has his own ministers of darkness that bring false sermons (2 Corinthians 11:4-5).
- Satan has formulated his own system of theology called "doctrines of demons" (1 Timothy 4:1 NASB; see also Revelation 2:24).
- Satan's ministers proclaim a counterfeit gospel—"a gospel other than the one we preached to you" (Galatians 1:7-8).
- Satan has his own throne (Revelation 13:2) and his own worshippers (13:4).
- Satan inspires false Christs and self-constituted messiahs (Matthew 24:4-5).
- Satan employs false teachers who bring in "destructive heresies" (2 Peter 2:1).
- Satan sends out false prophets (Matthew 24:11).
- Satan sponsors false apostles who imitate the true (2 Corinthians 11:13).

We have good reason to suspect that Satan is also counterfeiting dead humans in order to deceive the living. Demons are undoubtedly more than willing to masquerade as dead humans if they can deceive tens of millions of people and draw them away from Jesus Christ. As Ankerberg and Weldon note, "These spirits already know they will eventually be consigned forever to a place Jesus called hell (Matthew 8:29). The Scriptures lead us to conclude the real motive of the spirits is to take as many men to hell with them as possible by preventing their salvation (John 8:44; 2 Corinthians 11:3-4,13-14; Hebrews 2:14; 1 Peter 5:8)."[12]

The Dead Know They're Dead

The claim that the dead may not know they are dead might make for a good Hollywood movie like *The Sixth Sense,* but it has no basis in reality or the Bible. The rich man and Lazarus provide a good case in point. Both died, and both were fully aware that they were dead.

There was a rich man who was dressed in purple and fine linen and lived in luxury every day. At his gate was laid a beggar named Lazarus, covered with sores and longing to eat what fell from the rich man's table. Even the dogs came and licked his sores.

The time came when the beggar died and the angels carried him to Abraham's side. The rich man also died and was buried. In hell, where he was in torment, he looked up and saw Abraham far away, with Lazarus by his side. So he called to him, "Father Abraham, have pity on me and send Lazarus to dip the tip of his finger in water and cool my tongue, because I am in agony in this fire."

But Abraham replied, "Son, remember that in your lifetime you received your good things, while Lazarus received bad things, but now he is comforted here and you are in agony. And besides all this, between us and you a great chasm has been fixed, so that those who want to go from here to you cannot, nor can anyone cross over from there to us."

He answered, "Then I beg you, father, send Lazarus to my

father's house, for I have five brothers. Let him warn them, so that they will not also come to this place of torment."

Abraham replied, "They have Moses and the Prophets; let them listen to them."

"No, father Abraham," he said, "but if someone from the dead goes to them, they will repent."

He said to him, "If they do not listen to Moses and the Prophets, they will not be convinced even if someone rises from the dead" (Luke 16:19-31).

We learn several very important lessons in this passage of Scripture:

- Both the rich man and Lazarus had no doubt they had died and entered the afterlife.
- Once they died, their eternal destinies were sealed. Nothing could change their destinies. They had no second chance through reincarnation.
- Once they died, they could not stay on earth as ghosts.
- The dead and the living could not contact each other. A visitation to earth (in this case, to warn five brothers) was not an option.
- The righteous dead and wicked dead are separated, and the wicked are in torment. The Other Side is not equally wonderful for all people.

In this chapter, we have dispelled ghostly myths and focused needed attention on sound judgment and discernment. We have seen that many ghost reports are rooted in subjective experientialism (with no hard proof), a misinterpretation of the data, awakening from deep sleep, or fraudulence. When people encounter a genuine spirit, it is not a dead human but rather a demonic spirit intent on deceiving living humans. This assessment best explains all of the available data.

Next we begin our investigation into the paranormal world of psychics. We will have more myths to dispel and an ever-increasing need for sound judgment and discernment.

SIX

HOW PSYCHIC MEDIUMS OPERATE

P sychic mediums claim to communicate with dead people. Famous psychic mediums like James Van Praagh, John Edward, Sylvia Browne, and Char Margolis often do this on national TV. In fact, these individuals have made fortunes by their self-proclaimed ability to communicate with the dead. As we examine how these psychics actually do what they do, we will discover what is really going on.

First, let's look at the psychics' own claims about their methods of operation. Next we'll consider the allegations of critics. Finally, I'll give my personal assessment.

Psychics' Goal

James Van Praagh claims the spirits often want to make contact with the living in order to assure their living loved ones that they are okay. They can allegedly see their loved ones mourning over their deaths, so they want to bring comfort by conveying that death is not the end and that they are in a good place.[1]

Once living people hear from their dead relatives or friends through a psychic medium, Van Praagh claims, everything changes in their perspective. "With the knowledge of no death, they are free to live life. In an instant, a life overwrought with grief becomes a life ready to live each day and each moment with newness."[2] They are now at peace.

Van Praagh claims that "the biggest fear mankind has is of death. If we can abolish the fear of death, we can begin to live life to the fullest."[3] He claims, "Most people who come to me want closure with a loved one that has passed over or need proof that there is life after death. What I supply is the evidential detail. That's what helps them realize there is no death."[4]

Another reason the spirits often seek contact with the living, Van Praagh claims, is that they may personally be in need of forgiveness. They cannot rest peacefully or spiritually progress to the Other Side until earthly issues have been resolved. One of Van Praagh's goals is to help spirits seek and receive forgiveness for whatever wrongdoing they have committed during earthly life.[5]

Psychics Describe Their Methods

Psychic mediums consider themselves to be bridges between the physical world and the spiritual world. They claim their goal is to act as intermediaries between the living and the dead. This is easier said than done, they claim.[6]

The reason for this, psychics say, is that human beings on earth are composed of atoms and molecules that vibrate at a relatively slow rate because they are in physical bodies. By contrast, those in the spirit world (the Other Side) are allegedly composed of atoms and molecules that vibrate at a very fast speed. In order for the two worlds to communicate, spirits must slow their rapid vibrational rate while human psychic mediums must increase their slow vibrational rate.

John Edward provides an analogy. Though a helicopter has two to four blades, you cannot see them because they are spinning too fast. This is like the high vibrational rate of spirits. In contrast, a living human being's slow vibrational rate is like the blades of a slow-turning ceiling fan. You can see them clearly. During a psychic reading, Edward says, the spirit slows down its vibration as the psychic medium speeds his up. Communication allegedly takes place in the space between the two worlds.[7] Edward claims, "As I speed up and they slow down, across the great divide between our two worlds we meet somewhere in the middle and communicate."[8]

Edward claims that because of the space between the two worlds—a great gap—communication can be difficult. In the midst of this gap, spirits allegedly send psychic thoughts, feelings, and images, and the psychic medium's task is to interpret those thoughts, feelings, and images back to the living.[9]

One must keep in mind, Edward claims, that spirits no longer have physical bodies, including mouths, tongues, and vocal cords. They cannot enunciate words, so they send thoughts, feelings, and images. The psychic medium expresses these thoughts, feelings, and images to the living.[10]

Edward claims he goes through a series of exercises to help raise his vibrational rate. He begins by meditating, centering himself so that his "energies" are fully focused on the task at hand. As a Catholic, he also prays the rosary. He claims the spirits once showed him rosary beads turning into musical notes. He interpreted this as a symbolic message that the rosary is music to their ears. The rosary, Edward claims, brings us closer to the spirits and brings the spirits closer to us.

Van Praagh describes the process a bit differently. He claims that once the spirits slow their vibrational rate, they are able to send thoughts to the psychic medium telepathically.[11] He uses an analogy of a radio station to explain his concept:

> It's like a radio station...I actually will tune into, if you will, a certain energy. A frequency of the person's voice. I'm hearing their voice. And by hearing that voice, I receive impressions. Sometimes it's a scene of something. Sometimes it's a feeling of something. And I get words in front of me.[12]

Van Praagh says he can "turn off" when he so desires. "When I finish, I turn off the radio and take away any of that power of awareness."[13]

PSYCHIC SIGN LANGUAGE

Edward likens the thoughts, feelings, and images that come from spirits to psychic sign language. Often these thoughts, feelings, and images are symbolic. As psychic mediums become more fluent in understanding the symbols, Edward claims, they can more easily understand what the spirit is seeking to communicate.[14] For example, if Edward senses a tightness in his chest during a reading, he may interpret that as meaning that the person died from a heart attack. If Edward senses blackness in the chest area, he may interpret that as meaning that the person died of lung cancer.[15]

Edward says he never hears conversational language. He says people sometimes get the wrong idea that he is simply repeating what he has verbally heard from a spirit. In reality, he claims he is interpreting and delivering symbolic information as fast as he can keep up with it. "I get scenes in my head without the sound. I so wish I were hearing voices, but I don't. They're thoughts."[16]

Edward claims that if he were truly hearing conversational language, he would be a lot more accurate than he is.[17] He says mistakes in communication may happen because he is misinterpreting thoughts, feelings, and images. The primary message that comes through, however, is often quite clear: The spirit seeks to validate to living loved ones that he or she is okay so that these loved ones can be comforted and encouraged.

PSYCHIC SENSES

Psychic mediums often claim they utilize specific psychic senses to communicate with spirits. For example, John Edward claims he utilizes clairaudience, clairvoyance, clairsentience, clairalience, and clairhambience. I provided basic definitions of some of these terms in chapter 3.

Clairaudience. This word literally means "clear hearing." Just as dogs can hear higher frequencies than humans, psychic mediums claim to hear beyond the normal hearing range into the world of spirits. Edward says he can hear sounds, sometimes including voices, that come from spirits. Sometimes a psychic medium can hear only the voice of his mind. "Imagine that while you are reading this you are also thinking about whether or not you left the oven on. That's your mind's voice. That's how spirit messages sound to me."[18]

Clairvoyance. This term literally means "clear seeing." It is the alleged mental picturing of physical objects or events at a distance by psychic means. It includes the alleged ability to perceive things beyond physical reality—into the ethereal dimension, the realm of spirits. Edward claims he can see objects, symbols, and scenes communicated by spirits. These images may be literal (for example, the image of a car might point to a death in a car accident) or symbolic (for example, seeing a Ford might convey that the last name of a person is Ford). A psychic medium might claim to clairvoyantly see what a person looked like while on earth.[19]

Clairsentience. This literally means "clear sensing" or "clear feeling." It is the psychic medium's alleged ability to receive a projected emotion from nearby or from another (spiritual) dimension and experience that emotional sensation within his or her body. A psychic medium might claim to sense, for example, how a spirit feels now or how it felt prior to death and after. He or she might also claim to feel sympathetic pains—that is, if a person had joint pains while he was alive, a psychic medium might sense that pain during communication with the spirit.[20] Edward claims that if he is not correctly interpreting the feeling or emotion, it gradually feels bigger and bigger until he gets it right.[21]

Clairalience and clairhambience. *Clairalience* literally means "clear smelling." *Clairhambience* literally means "clear tasting." A psychic medium might claim to sense smells and tastes from a spirit. For example, a psychic medium might claim to smell something that was closely associated with the person while he was physically alive, such as a cigar.[22]

A combined sensory experience. Psychic mediums claim that accurately interpreting what a spirit is trying to communicate requires them to use these various psychic senses in concert with each other. They try to interpret the entire package—symbols, sounds, and feelings—into a single coherent message. Psychic mediums thus claim their work can be extremely draining.[23]

TELLING IT LIKE IT IS

Psychic mediums claim to never adjust or change messages they receive from spirits. They claim they do not edit communications from the dead, even if the information is personal or potentially embarrassing.[24] "Whatever I get, my client gets," Edward says. Psychics may, however, choose to put things in a kinder and gentler way. For example, if the psychic is perceiving a car accident that is yet future, the psychic might say to the client, "Be careful while you are driving."[25]

Allegations of Critics

We might get the feeling that psychic mediums genuinely contact dead humans and that their methods for doing so are highly refined. Later in the book, we will see that if psychic mediums are in communication with any spirits at all, they are in contact not with the dead but rather with demonic spirits. For now, however, I want to shift my attention to the allegations of critics regarding the way psychic mediums do what they do. Some of their findings are enlightening.

LET'S GO FISHING

Despite the rather elaborate psychic methodology we have mentioned, critics allege that many psychic mediums today *fish* for information during psychic readings as if they were playing 20 Questions. For example, a psychic might ask a studio audience something like this: "Do any of you have a relative whose name starts with *S?* Or *R?* Or maybe *D?*"

Sometimes, when throwing out letters that relate to a person's name, a psychic medium might mention that the letters could refer to a person either living or dead. This greatly increases the chances of a hit. Almost everyone knows someone else whose name begins with *S, R,* or *D.*

Or the psychic medium might say, "Are you going through a change in your life right now? I sense you're going through some kind of change." Almost everyone is going through some kind of change. Another common line goes like this: "I'm sensing a female figure. It's either a mom or a mother figure who has crossed over to the Other Side." It does not take a rocket scientist to recognize that a huge percentage of the American public has a mom or mother figure who has died.[26] Or the psychic medium might say, "I am sensing a male who is older than you." Everyone knows an older male who has died. Such lines are bound to generate significant response. Once the pschic has received a response—once he has hooked a person—he can then fish for other pertinent information.

Here is another line: "I sense that your grandmother has passed over and that you possess a piece of jewelry from her. I sense that this piece of jewelry is a closed circle." Of course, many people have a grandmother who has died. Moreover, a lot of people have jewelry from a dead relative. In most cases, the piece of jewelry is a closed circle—a ring, a necklace, or a bracelet.[27]

Psychic mediums may also fish for information about how a person died. For example, a psychic medium speaking to a client about the death of his father might say, "I'm sensing a pain in the chest area." If he receives a positive nod, he may ask if the father died of a heart attack. (Obviously, many people in the United States die of a heart attack.) If the psychic is wrong about a heart attack, he may say he senses a shadow in the body, and then ask if the father died of cancer. Or he might ask about the head area—perhaps a stroke or a head injury. Because heart attacks, cancer, strokes, and head injuries are statistically very common causes of death in our culture, the psychic stands a good chance of success of nailing a person's cause of death in this way.[28]

What all this means is that psychic mediums often ask leading questions that are statistically likely to elicit a response from many people, and once they get a response, they build on that information and run with it. This is often called a "cold reading" because the client walks in "cold," and the psychic has no advance information about the person (or persons, as is the case with a TV studio audience). While fishing for information, the psychic also pays attention to visual clues such as dress, body language, posture, and facial expressions. In such cold readings, the misses generally far outweigh the hits.

One factor that can greatly increase the chances of a hit is the size of the TV studio audience. A typical studio audience has about 200 people. If each person in the studio audience knows 50 other people (a conservative estimate), a potential pool of 10,000 people may relate to the question the psychic is asking. He is virtually certain to get some kind of response.[29] As one critic put it, "Edward's alleged psychic revelations have a high statistical probability of being true in the lives of many people."[30] The same is true of all psychic mediums who appear before studio audiences.

SCAMS AND FRAUDS

Some psychics are very clever. Every major psychic today has been accused of being a fraud. Are *their own* warnings about psychic scams and frauds intended to deflect attention away from themselves?

James Van Praagh, for example, warns his readers about psychic quacks: "If you plan on going to a psychic of any sort, or want a reading, always go by referral. Just like in every profession, there are people who are fakes and ones that are genuine."[31]

Char Margolis warns, "I'd be the last one to say that all psychics are the real thing. Of course there are people out there looking to make a quick buck or giving 'readings' from a desperate need for attention."[32]

Sylvia Browne says that psychics affiliated with psychic hotlines, 900 numbers, and those who run ads in newspapers are "scams" and "goofs."[33] She says, "It just makes you feel so bad because you just try to legitimize something that really is legitimate. You got all these goofs running around."[34]

Psychologists often say that people tend to condemn in others what they themselves are most guilty of. One must therefore wonder whether Van Praagh, Margolis, and Browne are seeking to legitimize themselves at the expense of other psychics. Certainly those who have studied the history of psychics have often claimed that this field is littered with cases of proven fraud. Investigators such as James Randi ("The Amazing Randi") and Christian illusionist Dan Korem (in his book, *The Fakers*) have provided substantive evidence for this. Faked psychic phenomena may include obtaining information beforehand (some psychics have been known to utilize the services of a private investigator), stage magic, and sleight-of-hand tricks.[35]

One of James Randi's first targets was psychic Uri Geller, tested by Stanford Research Institute for his alleged powers to bend spoons and levitate objects. Randi demonstrated that "the tricks were very simple...there was nothing you couldn't get off the back of a Corn Flakes box so to speak."[36]

Many years ago, magician Harry Houdini, in his book *A Magician Among the Spirits*, wrote this assessment:

> I have said many times that I am willing to believe, want to believe, will believe, if the Spiritualists can show any sub-stantiated proof, but until they do I shall have to live on, believing from all the evidence shown me and from what I have experienced that Spiritualism has not been proven satisfactory to the world at large and that none of the evidence offered has been able to stand up under the fierce rays of investigation.[37]

Not surprisingly, some of today's primetime psychics have been caught cheating. As James Van Praagh chatted with audience members prior to the taping of his show, he learned that one of the women in a particular area of the audience was from Italy. Later, after the cameras were rolling, he went over to that section and asked which person in that section was from another country. This looked to television viewers as if Van Praagh knew this informa-tion psychically, but he simply derived this information before the show even began.[38]

In another case, Van Praagh was filming a segment for ABC's

20/20. During a break, with the camera still rolling (unbeknownst to Van Praagh), he spoke with a woman and discovered that her grandmother had passed on. Within the next hour, while taping for the show, Van Praagh turned to the lady and said: "I want to tell you, there is a lady sitting behind you. She feels like a grandmother to me." When confronted about this by a *20/20* correspondent, Van Praagh defensively asserted, "I don't cheat. I don't have to prove... I don't cheat. I don't cheat. I mean, come on..."[39]

During the interview on *20/20,* Van Praagh made reference to Barbara Walter's father having a glass eye. Walters was impressed with this, noting that this is not public knowledge. However, the ABC reporter working on the story consulted a widely available book about Walters and quickly found a passage that explicitly stated that her father was blind in one eye and had a glass eye. He suggested that if he was able to uncover this information so easily, so could Van Praagh. Hugh Downs declared of Van Praagh, "I don't believe him."[40]

Audience members who participate on Van Praagh's TV show have to sign a release that states in part, "Neither anyone acting on my behalf, nor I...shall speak to any newspaper reporter, print or television journalist or other media representative or source about any aspect of my participation in the series." Apparently, Van Praagh doesn't want the media to know what really goes on during the taping of his shows. Could what goes on during the taping be much less impressive than the final edited version that appears on television?[41] One must wonder.

John Edward has also been caught cheating. On the popular news show *Dateline,* he tried to pass off as revelation information he had gained earlier in the day. While in alleged contact with some spirits, Edward said the spirits were telling him to "acknowledge Anthony." The cameraman indicated that was his name. Edward, with a surprised look on his face, said "That's you? Really?" Edward put on his actor's hat and gave a real show. But Anthony had been the cameraman on an earlier television show that same day with Edward. The two men had chatted, and Edward had obtained useful bits of information that he later pretended had come from the spirit realm. Edward was caught cheating.[42]

Tamara Rand is another fairly high-profile psychic who was caught cheating. Andre Kole and Terry Holley, in their book *Astrology and Psychic Phenomena*, explain:

> One of the best examples of deceit in the "psychic world" was perpetrated by Los Angeles "psychic" Tamara Rand. On April 2, 1981, just four days after the assassination attempt on President Ronald Reagan, the NBC television *Today* show, the ABC *Good Morning America show,* and the Cable News Network all broadcast a tape that was claimed to be made by Rand on January 6, 1981, in which she predicted Reagan would be shot in the chest by a man with the initials "J.H." during the last week of March or the first week of April. However, investigators found that the tape had been made Tuesday night, March 31, more than 24 hours after the assassination attempt.[43]

My Personal Assessment

Sometimes I talk to Christian critics of psychic mediums who say they're all a bunch of frauds. Case closed! I've spoken to others, however, who say nothing about fraudulent activity but rather conclude that all psychic mediums are in contact with demonic spirits. In my thinking, the combination of *both* fraudulent activity *and* demonic activity best explains what is really going on with psychics.

On the one hand, psychic mediums undoubtedly often utilize a fishing technique to derive information from clients. One need only observe a psychic session to see this is true. Moreover, some psychic mediums have clearly cheated, pretending to derive certain information from heaven when in reality they derived it prior to the session. Based on what I've been able to discover, I would guesstimate that well over half of what goes on among psychic mediums is fraudulent in some way.

On the other hand, we should not conclude that all psychic

phenomena involves hoaxes. Psychics sometimes make genuine contact with spirit entities—but the spirit entities are not departed human beings, as psychics claim, but rather *demonic* spirits.[44] My former colleague Walter Martin is correct in warning that "there are many Christians, unfortunately, who suffer from the illusion that all Spiritism, or spiritistic evidence, is fraudulent, and prefer to rest in the falsely secure belief that Spiritism can never be demonically empowered."[45] Martin also asserts, "Not *all* psychic or spiritistic phenomena can be exposed as fraudulent. There is a spiritual dimension that cannot be ignored. Authentic spiritists draw their power from the one the Bible calls 'a roaring lion' who seeks 'whom he may devour' (1 Peter 5:8 KJV), who is Satan."[46]

Let us not forget that in 2 Corinthians 11:14 the apostle Paul sternly warned that "Satan himself masquerades as an angel of light." Many apologists infer from this that in many cases with psychic mediums, Satan and his horde of demons (fallen angels) may be mimicking dead people. They do so for a malevolent, sinister purpose—to lead people away from the true Christ and God of the Bible. In the process of doing this, they propagate doctrines of demons (1 Timothy 4:1-3 NASB). These doctrines of demons include ideas like these: Death is not to be feared; all people go to heaven, regardless of religion; and the dead can communicate with the living (see chapter 8: "Doctrines of Demons").

This connection to Satan may also explain some of the fraudulent activity of psychics. Inasmuch as psychics are deeply engulfed in occultism and are trafficking with Satan and his host of demons, they would be likely to take on the character of these fallen spirits. More to the point, John 8:44, speaking of Satan, tells us, "There is no truth in him. When he lies, he speaks his native language, for he is a liar and the father of lies." Satan is a deceiver, and his deception may be reflected in those who serve his dark kingdom—psychics, mediums, and other occultists. If they are empowered by him, they will probably reflect his nature.

I agree with former psychic and occultist Marcia Montenegro, who is careful to emphasize that we should not succumb to an either-or mentality when interpreting the work of psychic mediums. "The issue is often framed in terms of 'either-or.' *Either* the mediums are frauds *or* they are receiving information from spirits; but must it be one or the other?"[47] Famous psychics such as James Van Praagh, Sylvia Browne, John Edward, and Char Margolis may in some cases fish for information and at other times even cheat by deriving information beforehand. But at other times they may be in genuine contact with demonic spirit entities. These are truly times for discernment.

SEVEN

ASSESSING THE ACCURACY OF PSYCHIC MEDIUMS

P sychics claim that no psychic is 100 percent accurate 100 percent of the time. Such a statement, however, carries with it the implication that they are largely accurate most of the time. Let's look at the facts regarding the accuracy of psychics.

The sad reality of our day is that many people, especially those who are grieving and desperately seeking communication with their dead loved ones, seem more than willing to overlook significant misses on the part of psychics. If mourners have any chance to reach their dead loved ones, they seem to permit any number of misses.

The Track Record of Psychics

The history of psychics' predictions is a target-rich environment. Space prohibits a detailed listing of such failures, but even the little that I document below provides more than sufficient evidence for their dismal track record.

9/11 AND CHALLENGER
The predictions psychics made for 2001 are highly revealing. All psychics, bar none, failed to foresee what must be considered

the most important and defining event of 2001: the terrorist attacks against the Twin Towers in New York City. Had any of them foreseen this event, they could have helped save thousands of lives.

As you might expect, many people have confronted psychics about their failure to predict this event. Most of the psychics provide a revisionist account of what happened.

For example, in 2003—long after the 2001 tragedy occurred—James Van Praagh claimed he had been visiting in Greece with a friend when he suddenly turned to him and said, "Oh my gosh, there's going to be a horrible situation." His friend asked him what he meant. "Well, I see smoke and fire and glass on the East Coast." He claims he said, "There'll be thousands of lives that are going to be lost. I don't know what it is. I just don't know what it is." He claims he felt bad that this tragedy was going to happen, but because he didn't know the exact location, he was unable to do anything about it.[1]

Notice two important facts here:

- Van Praagh did not speak publicly about this tragedy prior to 2001. He spoke about it in retrospect later. One cannot help but suspect that his retrospect account is pure revisionism.
- Van Praagh says he did not know the exact location where the tragedy would take place. He claims he was not given this information by the spirits. This omission from the spirit world serves to insulate Van Praagh from criticism for not warning people in the Twin Towers.

Revisionism is also suspected in regard to the space shuttle Challenger that blew up in 1986. Van Praagh claims, "I was ironing my shirt getting ready for work and I was watching that takeoff and I said, 'Oh my gosh, it's going to blow up.' And then within five minutes it took off and blew up."[2] Notice two things here:

- Van Praagh claims he was only given five minutes advance notice of the tragedy. This timing makes it impossible for him to have gone public with this knowledge so that the tragedy might have been averted.

• Van Praagh speaks of this alleged premonition of disaster in retrospect. Again, one cannot help but suspect that this is pure revisionism.

FAILED PREDICTIONS FOR 2004

A look at some of psychic Sylvia Browne's predictions for 2004 is highly revealing. In December 2003, she made these assertions on *The Montel Williams Show:*

• Our American troops will be pulled out of Iraq by June or July, 2004.
• Osama bin Laden will be "dead as a doornail" in 2004.
• Martha Stewart will not go to jail.
• North Korea will launch nuclear weapons.[3]

In earlier years, Browne predicted that Bill Clinton would be vindicated in the Monica Lewinsky scandal. She also predicted that Bill Bradley would win the 2000 U.S. presidential election with the Reform Party coming in second.[4]

FAILED PREDICTIONS FOR 2005

Psychics made widely publicized predictions for 2005 that did not pan out. Here are a few of the major misses:

• Saddam Hussein will be assassinated in 2005.
• Public elections in Iraq will result in the United States pulling out of Iraq in 2005.
• A massive earthquake will occur in the southwest United States.
• The Giants will win the series against Cleveland in game seven.

MORE RECENT FAILURES

Sylvia Browne's alleged psychic knowledge of the late-2005 West Virginia miners' tragedy was also incorrect. She was a guest on George Noory's live syndicated radio show, *Coast to Coast*, when she had the bad luck to be commenting on a developing news story that took a surprise turn. The tragic twist—a wrong announcement had been broadcast about the miners' fate—turned out to be even worse news for Browne. Here's what happened:

Noory bought up the mining disaster, and Browne seemed relieved to hear from him that all but one of the miners were alive. Noory then asked Browne, "Had you been on the program earlier today, would you have felt if—because they heard no sound—that this was a very gloomy moment—and that they might have all died?" Browne responded, "No. I knew they were going to be found."

Shortly thereafter, however, Noory received updated information and reported that all but one of the miners had been killed. This rude awakening for Browne caused her to hedge and backtrack: "I don't think there's anybody alive, maybe one. How crazy for them to report that they were all alive when they weren't!...I just don't think they are alive." At this point, Browne cleared her throat, and there was a deafening pause. Noory went to a commercial break.

After returning from the commercial, Noory tried to help Browne recover by asking a question on an unrelated matter. But Browne—desperate to rescue her marred image—suddenly interrupted and blurted out, "I didn't believe that they were all alive." Noory said, "What's that, the miners?" Browne said, "Yeah, I didn't think—and see, I've been on the show with you, but I don't think there's any that are going to make it."[5]

Edited for Primetime

Some may wonder why psychics, on their own television shows, appear to be so accurate. Let us consider John Edward as an example. His television show, *Crossing Over,* was a huge hit on the Sci-Fi channel.

Each half-hour episode of *Crossing Over* requires six hours of taping. Why? One critic says the editors of the program carefully plucked successes from a whole mass of misses that happened during the show.[6]

A visitor who attended John Edward's *Crossing Over* claims his interaction with Edward on the show was edited to make Edward look good. The visitor claims that only a fraction of what took place in the studio actually made its way into the final 30-minute broadcast. Edward was wrong about a lot of things, the guest claims, and those errors were all omitted from the broadcast.[7]

The guest also alleges that Edward's production assistants were always around while people waited to get into the studio, and he claims they easily could have overheard a lot. Further, once in the studio, audience members had to wait for nearly two hours before the show taping began. "Throughout that time everybody was talking about what dead relative of theirs might pop up. Remember that all this occurred under microphones and cameras already set up." The visitor speculates that perhaps some of Edward's staff was listening backstage and taking notes. When Edward finally appeared, the visitor claims Edward was looking at audience members as if he were trying to spot someone he recognized.[8]

Edward, understandably, denies all this. Yes, he says, the show *is* edited—but only for time, not for content. He says their editing is done so as to not produce false impressions. Producers do not manipulate the facts, he says. "From day one, I was very concerned that we not edit the show so that all the invalidated information and slower moments disappeared, essentially leaving a highlight reel of one jaw-dropping read after another." He says that editing *Crossing Over* in a way that distorts what actually occurred is not something he could go along with.[9] He also claims that such allegations are a real insult to the integrity and professionalism of his staff on the show.[10] Still, Edward has been caught cheating before, and all genuine psychic activity comes from the father of lies (John 8:44), so one cannot help but wonder.

What If a Psychic Is Accurate?

What if a psychic's prediction turns out to be accurate? What then? I would suggest the following points to add perspective:

- An occasional hit in a sea of misses is not impressive.

- Some hits are due to the cards being stacked in the psychic's favor—such as a psychic predicting continued Palestinian hostility toward Israel or an earthquake in California. Such things are bound to occur.
- Don't discount the possibility of the psychic having gained inside information somehow. Psychics have been caught cheating in the past!
- In some cases, a demonic spirit could communicate accurate paranormal knowledge to a psychic. In this case, the demon may impersonate a benevolent spirit guide or perhaps a dead human (2 Corinthians 11:14) and communicate accurate paranormal knowledge in order to give credence to the false religion of Spiritualism, thereby drawing people away from the truth of the Bible. I believe this explains any genuine hits by psychics.

Excuses, Excuses!

When psychics make a wrong prediction or offer inaccurate information during a psychic reading, they seem to always have an excuse ready at hand. For people who are already open to psychic phenomena, such excuses may seem convincing. But to objective critics who are interested only in facts, such excuses are less than convincing. Here are some of the more common excuses.

MISTAKES AND "TRICKSTER ENERGY"

When Char Margolis appeared on *Larry King Live*, she made a number of obvious errors. Covering herself, she said these errors may be due to "trickster energy."[11] Evidently this means that prankster spirits exist who take delight in playing tricks on psychics.

INFORMATION FOR SOMEONE ELSE

James Van Praagh and John Edward also had some major misses on *Larry King Live*. When Van Praagh made one particular error, both he and Edward suggested that the information must be meant for someone in the listening audience, a friend, coworker, or relative, someone in another building nearby, or perhaps someone in the past or in the future, known or unknown. With this kind of latitude, psychics can apparently never be wrong.[12]

SYMBOLIC COMMUNICATION

Psychics sometimes claim that one reason for their inaccuracy is that spirits often communicate in symbols, and such symbols are difficult to interpret. Edward admits, "I might be interpreting the information incorrectly...I'm shown images by the Other Side that could take on a number of meanings, and my immediate interpretation is one meaning when it's actually another."[13] On the one hand, this admission by Edward makes him appear humble, thus endearing him to his audience. On the other hand, the excuse serves as a loophole that he can appeal to—anytime, any day—to explain away any inaccurate data he gives. Any way you look at it, Edward comes out looking fine regardless of his mistakes.

SPIRITS' LIMITATIONS

In some cases, a client might be seeking information from spirits regarding such things as wealth, romance, or one's career. However, Van Praagh says that the spirits might not be able to provide such information. On the one hand, the spirit may simply not know the information one is seeking. On the other hand, the spirit may know the information but not be permitted to reveal it. As Van Praagh puts it, "When a soul comes on this earth to learn certain lessons or to spiritually progress, the last thing he or she needs is for a spirit being to give the answers to a situation that may be a test." Van Praagh says spirits are subject to spiritual laws and are not permitted to interfere or influence the spiritual or karmic progression of a living person on earth. What this means, practically speaking, is that certain information must remain veiled to living human beings.[14] This too is a loophole excuse that psychics can appeal to—anytime, any day—when they are unable to provide helpful information to clients.

UNINVITED SPIRITS

Edward says that in certain cases, clients desire to hear from one particular individual, but a different spirit speaks from the Other Side, and the client decides that psychic contact is bogus. For example, clients might want to make contact with a rich uncle so the location of the family stash can be discovered, but instead they hear from someone who had a crush on them in high school. "When this happens, it doesn't matter how hard the energies or I work to open your eyes—nothing will make you see. And then you go home disappointed, assuming that the process just 'didn't work' for you."[15]

Audience members of *Crossing Over* are coached before they even enter into the television studio regarding how they should behave during taping. Here is an exerpt from the audience rules on the *Crossing Over* website:

> Have no expectations. You may really want to connect with one specific relative…but there is a good chance they may not come through. Keep your mind open and welcome whoever comes through during the reading. We don't want you to be disappointed or brokenhearted if your chosen loved one doesn't come through. As John says, "Please do not put earthly expectations on a heavenly experience."[16]

This excuse serves to diffuse disappointment before it (inevitably) takes place.

PEOPLE CHANGE

Psychics often describe dead loved ones in ways that seem foreign to the memories of the living. This causes some clients to suspect that the psychic is not really in contact with their dead loved ones.

Psychics respond by claiming that people undergo changes once they cross over to the Other Side. Edward suggests that when a person dies, he or she sheds the human body along with all worldly limitations. Physical weaknesses are gone. Emotional burdens dissolve.

Our negative aspects soften, and our positive aspects become highlighted. "It's like the worm going into the cocoon, shedding skin, and becoming the butterfly. We are that worm as we move through life, and one day we become that butterfly when our physical body dies, allowing our soul to soar."[17] For this reason, psychics advise their clients not to expect their loved ones to be exactly as they were while alive on earth. This is a very handy excuse because psychics often get personal details wrong about those on the Other Side.

MISSING INFORMATION

Edward claims that in some cases, clients may not know whether or not the information is correct simply because they are ignorant of certain relevant data. For example, a client might be ignorant or unfamiliar with his or her own family tree. In such a case, the psychic might refer to a relative that the client is unaware he or she has.[18] The client might claim the psychic is wrong, but he really is not.

PSYCHIC AMNESIA

Sometimes, psychics are allegedly accurate, but—for whatever reason—clients experience some kind of psychic amnesia and do not remember normally memorable names or events, such as a spouse's name or the date of a child's birthday.[19] When psychics relay information related to issues clients have forgotten, clients may claim the information is wrong or inaccurate. (This is one of the most bizarre excuses I've come across.)

What About Lotteries and the Stock Market?

Sometimes critics like to ask psychics two questions:

- Why haven't you used your psychic abilities to win the lottery?
- Why haven't you used your psychic abilities to cash in with investments in the stock market?

Not unexpectedly, psychics have an answer. Sylvia Browne, for example, says that genuine psychics are not psychic about themselves. "God generously gave us a gift, not to hoard or waste on lottery numbers...but to turn around and give to everyone else just as generously."[20] The psychic gift is allegedly given to bless others. If the gift is abused, Browne says, psychics deserve to lose it. So Browne's gift is intended to bless people, but of course, these people have to pay Browne $750 per session to get blessed!

The Million-Dollar Offer

I love contests! I don't think I could come up with a better contest than to offer $1 million to any person who can objectively prove his or her psychic abilities. James Randi—longtime debunker of psychics—has set up such a contest. Regarding the million-dollar offer, Randi promised this on the March 6, 2001, *Larry King Live* show: "A million dollars in negotiable bonds, Larry, to any person or persons who can provide evidence of any paranormal, occult, or supernatural event or ability of any kind under proper observing conditions. It is that simple."[21]

During the March 6, 2001, *Larry King Live* show, Sylvia Browne agreed to take Randi's $1 million paranormal challenge. Unfortunately, she failed to follow through.

On the September 3, 2001, *Larry King Live* show, Browne again committed to taking the test. Again, she failed to follow through.

When Browne appeared on *Larry King Live* on May 16, 2003, a caller asked Sylvia why she had agreed to take Randi's $1 million paranormal challenge and yet failed to follow through. Brown gave the excuse that Randi would not put the money into escrow. On the show, she subsequently agreed to take the test if the money could be validated.

The money *was* validated. Randi even sent a letter to Browne documenting proof of the money. The letter was refused and sent back to the sender. One can only deduce that Browne never intended to take the challenge in the first place. The reason seems obvious. Her reputation would be ruined because she would surely fail the test.

After the continued embarrassment of refusing Randi's $1 million challenge, Browne put up a note at her website claiming that she answers to God alone, and she is accountable to no one else for her gift. She said, "I have no interest in your $1 million or any intention of pursuing it." She then went on to suggest that this money be donated to a legitimate charity, such as the Multiple Sclerosis Foundation, The American Red Cross, or The Salvation Army.[22]

Randi wonders about Browne's inconsistency. First, Browne insisted on proof of the money's existence. Later, she asserted that she was not interested in the money.[23] Both statements seem to be motivated by a desire to avoid being objectively tested.

To date, Randi continues to offer his million-dollar prize to Browne or anyone else who gives proof of miraculous psychic ability. So far, no one has accepted.

Predictions for the Future

Quite a number of psychics have made predictions for the future. Sylvia Browne's are especially notable. Here are a few things she predicts:

- Cancer will be eradicated. (Doctors are continually working on eradicating cancer, so paranormal insight is not required to guess that one day they will succeed.)
- Computers will control robotic houses. (Microsoft founder Bill Gates already utilizes computer technology to control many aspects of his house. Guessing that one day such houses may be commonplace does not require paranormal insight.)
- Separate body parts will be cloned for organ transplants. (Surely Browne is aware that geneticists have discussed such a possibility for years. No paranormal insight is needed here. Currently, however, the ethics of such cloning is still being debated.)
- The West Coast will go underwater by 2026. (We all know "the big one" is going to hit some time. It may or

may not happen by 2026. In any event, no paranormal insight is needed to guess this eventuality.)[24]

Compared with the true God of the Bible, psychics simply cannot deliver. As the prophet Daniel said, "No wise man, enchanter, magician or diviner can explain to the king the mystery he has asked about, but there is a God in heaven who reveals mysteries" (Daniel 2:27-28), for it is God who alone has all wisdom and power, who reveals deep and mysterious things and knows what lies hidden in darkness, though He Himself is surrounded by light (Daniel 2:20,22).[25]

EIGHT

DOCTRINES OF DEMONS

The apostle John instructs his readers, "Do not believe every spirit, but test the spirits to see whether they are from God, because many false prophets have gone out into the world" (1 John 4:1). Even in John's day, many false prophets were energized by demonic spirits.

The question understandably arose, how can Christians distinguish true prophets from false prophets? How can Christians detect whether the source of the prophet's message is the Holy Spirit or a demonic spirit?

The solution was to "test the spirits." In other words, as prophets delivered the teachings of spirits, believers were to test them against the Word of God. Anything that disagreed with God's Word came from an evil spirit, for the Holy Spirit never inspires doctrinal error and never inspires anything that contradicts God's Word.

Today, we test the spirits in the same way. More specifically, we test the doctrinal teachings of psychics—teachings derived from the Other Side—against the Word of God. When we encounter teachings contrary to God's Word, the spirits speaking through the psychics clearly are not of God but are rather evil spirits seeking to deceive us.

Let's measure specific doctrinal teachings from the psychics against the Word of God. We'll see that the source of such psychic teachings cannot be God but rather must be demonic spirits intent on communicating "doctrines of demons" (1 Timothy 4:1-3 NASB). By the time we are finished, we will see that Sylvia Browne, John Edward, and Char Margolis are utterly misguided in their assertion that their psychic gift is from the Holy Spirit or from God.

The Bible

The Psychic View

The Bible should not be interpreted literally, for such an interpretation will lead people astray. The Bible should be interpreted esoterically—that is, spiritually—to discover hidden spiritual truths in Scripture.[1]

The Christian View

An esoteric (spiritualized) method of interpreting Scripture is illegitimate for at least seven reasons:

1. Esotericism violates the Scriptural injunction to rightly handle the Word of God and not distort its meaning. Some people distort Scripture "to their own destruction" (2 Peter 3:16). Contrary to this, we should avoid distorting God's Word and should set forth God's truth plainly (2 Corinthians 4:2). We should correctly handle the Word of truth (2 Timothy 2:15).

2. In esotericism, the basic authority in interpretation is not Scripture but rather the mind of the interpreter. Because of this, esoteric interpreters come up with radically different (and contradictory) meanings of specific Bible verses. Such contradictions are inevitable when the authority is the interpreter's mind and not Scripture.

3. Esoteric interpreters rely on their own inner illumination to determine what Scripture means, whereas Christians rely on the Holy Spirit for illumination. Scripture indicates that full comprehension of the Word of God is impossible without prayerful dependence on the Spirit of God (1 Corinthians 2:9-11), for He

who inspired the Word (2 Peter 1:21) is also its supreme interpreter (John 16:12-15).

4. Esotericism superimposes mystical meanings onto Bible verses instead of objectively seeking the biblical author's intended meaning. We ought to put nothing into the Scriptures but rather draw everything from them. What a passage means is fixed by the author and is not subject to alteration by readers. "Meaning is *determined* by the author; it is *discovered* by readers."[2]

5. Esotericism ignores the context of Bible verses. Every word in the Bible is part of a verse, and every verse is part of a paragraph, and every paragraph is part of a book. No verse of Scripture is independent from the verses around it. The overall context is critical to properly interpreting Bible verses.

6. Esotericism ignores grammar, history, and culture. If we ignore grammar, history, and culture, how can we possibly hope to ascertain the author's intended meaning? Bible scholar Gordon Lewis says, "When we claim biblical authority for an idea, we must be prepared to show from the grammar, the history, the culture and the context that the writer in fact taught that idea. Otherwise the Bible is not *used* but *abused*."[3]

7. Esotericism goes against the example set by Jesus Christ in how to properly interpret Scripture. Jesus never interpreted the Old Testament Scriptures esoterically. On the contrary, He interpreted events in the Old Testament quite literally, including the creation account of Adam and Eve (Matthew 13:35; 25:34; Mark 10:6), Noah's ark and the flood (Matthew 24:38-39; Luke 17:26-27), Jonah and the great fish (Matthew 12:39-41), Sodom and Gomorrah (Matthew 10:15), and the account of Lot and his wife (Luke 17:28-29). Jesus' interpretation of Scripture was always in accord with the grammatical and historical meaning.

Would psychics say Jesus was wrong in this? If so, then why do they call Him enlightened? If Jesus was not wrong, then why don't psychics follow His enlightened example?

Jesus Christ

The Psychic View

Psychics consistently deny the absolute deity of Jesus Christ as well as His bodily resurrection from the dead. He is not unique but rather enlightened and divine in the sense that all people are enlightened and divine. Just as Jesus embodied the Christ, so all people can embody the Christ. Sylvia Browne says it does not matter if Jesus is the Son of God because all human beings are the Son of God.[4]

The Christian View

The biblical view is that Jesus is absolute deity. His deity is proved by the names the Bible ascribes to Him, including God (Hebrews 1:8), Lord (Matthew 22:43-44), and King of kings and Lord of lords (Revelation 19:16). He also has all the attributes of deity, including omnipotence (Matthew 28:18), omniscience (John 1:48), omnipresence (Matthew 18:20), and immutability (Hebrews 13:8). Further, He did things only God can do, such as creating the entire universe (Colossians 1:16; John 1:3). Still further, people worshipped Him as God many times according to the Gospel accounts. He accepted worship from Thomas (John 20:28), the angels (Hebrews 1:6), some wise men (Matthew 2:11), a leper (Matthew 8:2), a ruler (Matthew 9:18), a blind man (John 9:38), an anonymous woman (Matthew 15:25), Mary Magdalene (Matthew 28:9), and the disciples (Matthew 28:17). The fact that Jesus willingly received (and condoned) worship on various occasions says a lot about His true identity, for Scripture consistently testifies that only God can be worshipped (Exodus 34:14).

Jesus is also uniquely the Christ (that is, no one else is the Christ, as psychics claim). When the angel announced the birth of Jesus to the shepherds, he identified Jesus this way: "Today in the town of David a Savior has been born to you; he is Christ the Lord" (Luke 2:11). Jesus did not *become* the Christ as an adult but rather was the one and only Christ from the very beginning. John's first epistle thus warns us, "Who is the liar? It is the man who denies that Jesus is the Christ. Such a man is the antichrist—he denies the Father and the Son" (1 John 2:22).

The Old Testament presents hundreds of prophecies about the single Messiah (for example, Isaiah 7:14; 53:3-5; Micah 5:2; Zechariah 12:10). The New Testament counterpart of the Old Testament word for *Messiah* is *Christ* (see John 1:41). Jesus alone fulfilled these hundreds of prophecies, so He alone is the Christ.

Significantly, when people acknowledged Jesus as the Christ in the New Testament, He never said, "You too have the Christ within." Instead He warned that others would come falsely claiming to be the Christ (Matthew 24:5).

Finally, contrary to the psychics, Jesus did in fact bodily rise from the dead. The evidence for the resurrection is convincing:

- The resurrected Christ said: "See My hands and My feet, that it is I Myself; touch Me and see, for a spirit does not have flesh and bones as you see that I have" (Luke 24:39 NASB). Notice three things here: (1) The resurrected Christ indicates in this verse that He is not a spirit, (2) He indicates that His resurrection body is made up of flesh and bones, and (3) Christ's physical hands and feet represent physical proof of the materiality of His resurrection from the dead.
- The resurrected Christ ate physical food on four different occasions. He did this as a means of proving that He had a real physical body (Luke 24:30; 24:42-43; John 21:12-13; Acts 1:4).
- People handled and touched the resurrected Christ's physical body (Matthew 28:9; Luke 24:39; John 20:17).
- Five hundred people saw the physically resurrected Christ at a single time (1 Corinthians 15:6).
- Too many people saw the physically resurrected Christ on too many different occasions over too long a time (Acts 1:3) for His physical resurrection to be glibly dismissed, as psychics do. History is on the side of the resurrection.

God

The Psychic View

Some psychics, such as Jach Pursel and J.Z. Knight, believe in pantheism—the idea that God is all and all is God.[5] In this viewpoint, God is not a personal being but rather an impersonal force. "We express our belief in a supreme Impersonal Power, everywhere-present, manifesting as life, to all forms of organized matter, called by some, God; by others, Spirit; and by Spiritualists, Infinite Intelligence."[6]

Other psychics, such as Sylvia Browne, hold to both a Father God and a Mother God (Azna). She says Azna "is the counterpart of the Father, worshipped as His equal and His complement for more than twenty thousand years." The Father God is characterized by intellect whereas the Mother God is characterized by emotion.[7]

The Christian View

The pantheistic doctrine that "God is all" is unbiblical and has numerous critical problems. First, it destroys all distinctions between creation (which is finite) and the Creator (who is infinite). As Norman Geisler put it, "all alleged I-thou or I-I relations reduce to I."[8] In the biblical perspective, God is eternally distinct from what He created. God, who is infinite and eternal, created all things out of absolute nothingness (Hebrews 11:3; see also Genesis 1:1; Nehemiah 9:6; Psalm 33:8-9; 148:5). God is omnipresent (Psalm 139:7-9), but He is not pantheistically "one with" the universe. He remains eternally distinct from creation and from humankind (see Numbers 23:19; Ecclesiastes 5:2; Hebrews 11:3).

Further, the psychic view fails to adequately deal with the existence of real evil in the world. If God is the essence of all life forms in creation, then one must conclude that both good and evil stem from one and the same essence (God). Contrary to this, the God of the Bible is light, and "in Him is no darkness at all" (1 John 1:5; see also Habakkuk 1:13; Matthew 5:48). First John 1:5 is particularly cogent in the Greek, which translates literally, "And darkness there is not in Him, not in any way." John could not have said it more forcefully.

Related to this is Isaiah's warning: "Woe to those who call evil good, and good evil" (Isaiah 5:20). Saying that good and evil stem from the same essence of God is the same as calling evil good and calling good evil.

Contrary to the view that God is an impersonal force, the Bible indicates that God is a person. More specifically, God is a conscious being who thinks, feels, and purposes, and He carries His purposes into action. A person engages in active relationships with others. You can talk to a person and get a response. You can share feelings and ideas with him. You can argue with him, love him, and even hate him. By this definition, God must be understood as a person.

The Bible presents God as a loving Father to whom believers may cry, "Abba" (Mark 14:36; Romans 8:15; Galatians 4:6). "Abba" is an Aramaic term of great intimacy, loosely meaning "daddy." Jesus often spoke of God as a loving Father. Indeed, God is the personal "Father of compassion" of all believers (2 Corinthians 1:3). Walter Martin sheds further light on the personal nature of God:

> This Almighty Person performs acts that only a personality is capable of: God hears (Exodus 2:24); God sees (Genesis 1:4); God creates (Genesis 1:1); God knows (2 Timothy 2:19; Jeremiah 29:11); God has a will (1 John 2:17)... This is the God of Christianity, an omnipotent, omniscient, and omnipresent Personality, who manifests every attribute of personality.[9]

Finally, the Bible knows no second God called "Mother God." The consistent testimony of Scripture from Genesis to Revelation points to only one true God. This thread runs through every page of the Bible. God affirmed through Isaiah the prophet, "This is what the LORD says—Israel's King and Redeemer, the LORD Almighty: I am the first and I am the last; apart from me there is no God" (Isaiah 44:6). God also said, "I am God, and there is no other; I am God, and there is none like me" (46:9). The New Testament similarly emphasizes God's oneness. In 1 Corinthians 8:4, for example, the apostle Paul asserted that "there is no God but one." James 2:19 says, "You believe that there is one God. Good! Even the demons believe that—and shudder." These and a multitude of other verses (including John 5:44; 17:3; Romans 3:29-30; 16:27; Galatians 3:20; Ephesians 4:6; and 1 Timothy 2:5) make absolutely clear that there is one and *only* one God.

Humanity

The Psychic View

Psychics say human beings are perfect in their nature and are one with God. James Van Praagh says, "I believe we are all God... We are all made in the likeness of God...We are all made of the God spark...Each one of us is perfect if we would only seek our divinity."[10]

The Christian View

If the essence of human beings is God, and if God is an infinite, changeless being, then how is it possible for man (if he is a manifestation of divinity) to go through a changing process of enlightenment by which he discovers his divinity, as psychics teach? The fact that a man comes to realize he is God proves that he is not God. For if he were God he would never have passed from a state of ignorance to a state of awareness as to his divinity.[11] God does not blossom; He is always in full bloom.

Further, if all people possessed a part of the divine essence and were all manifestations of God, they would display qualities similar to God's. This seems only logical. However, when one compares the attributes of humankind with those of God (as set forth in Scripture), we find more than ample testimony for the truth of Paul's statement in Romans 3:23 that human beings "fall short of the glory of God."

- God is all-knowing (Matthew 11:21), but man is limited in knowledge (Job 38:4).
- God is all-powerful (Revelation 19:6), but man is weak (Hebrews 4:15).

- God is everywhere-present (Psalm 139:7-12), but man is confined to a single space at a time (for example, John 1:50).
- God is holy (1 John 1:5), but even man's righteous deeds are as filthy garments before God (Isaiah 64:6).
- God is eternal (Psalm 90:2), but man was created at a point in time (Genesis 1:1,21,27).
- God is truth (John 14:6), but man's heart is deceitful above all else (Jeremiah 17:9).
- God is characterized by justice (Acts 17:31), but man is lawless (1 John 3:4; see also Romans 3:23).
- God is love (Ephesians 2:4-5), but man is plagued with numerous vices like jealousy and strife (1 Corinthians 3:3).

If man is a god, one could never tell it by his attributes!

Still further, if human beings are God, why do they so powerfully sense their inferiority in His presence? When Isaiah found himself in God's presence, he cried out, "Woe is me, for I am ruined!... I am a man of unclean lips... For my eyes have seen the King, the LORD of hosts" (Isaiah 6:5 NASB). Similarly, when John had a vision on the Isle of Patmos and beheld the glorified Christ, he said: "When I saw Him, I fell at His feet as a dead man" (Revelation 1:17 NASB). Something about seeing God as He really is has an indescribable effect on people. It is the height of human arrogance to even toy with the idea that human beings are divine.

Sin and Salvation

The Psychic View

Psychics claim sin does not exist. Sin is an illusion. Man is not morally fallen. There is no offense to God that needs fixing.[12] Consequently, psychics claim human beings do not need to be saved. A spirit entity named Seth, communicating through psychic medium Jane Roberts, said, "The soul is not something you must save or redeem."[13] A spirit named Ramtha, communicating through psychic medium J.Z. Knight, said, "The world doesn't need saving—leave it alone...Relinquish guilt...Do not live by rules, live by feelings."[14] A spirit called Jesus, communicating through psychic medium Helen Schucman, said, "It is a terrible misconception that God Himself judged His own son on behalf of salvation... It is so essential that all such thinking be dispelled that we must be sure that nothing of this kind remains in your mind."[15]

The Christian View

The biblical Jesus taught that people have a grave sin problem that is altogether beyond their means to solve (Matthew 12:34; Luke 11:13). He taught that people are by nature evil and that they are capable of great wickedness (Mark 7:20-23; Luke 11:42-52). He said people are utterly lost (Luke 19:10), are sinners (Luke 15:10), and are in need of repentance before a holy God (Mark 1:15).

Jesus often spoke of human sin with metaphors that illustrate the havoc sin can wreak in one's life. He described human sin as a blindness (Matthew 15:14; 23:16-26), a sickness (Matthew 9:12), being enslaved in bondage (John 8:34), and living in darkness (John 3:19-21; 8:12; 12:35-46). He also taught that this is a universal condition and that all people are guilty before God (see Luke 7:37-48). Moreover, He taught that external acts aren't the only things that render a person guilty of sin; inner thoughts do as well (Matthew 5:28).

So human beings are in need of salvation in the worst sort of way. This salvation is found not by enlightenment but by placing faith in Jesus Christ (John 3:16; Acts 16:31), who Himself is the Light of the world (John 8:12) and the Savior of humankind (Titus 2:13-14). And the present life is the only opportunity we have to place faith in Him (that is, there is no second chance through reincarnation). We live once, die once, and then face the judgment (Hebrews 9:27). For this reason, the apostle Paul said, "Now is the day of salvation" (2 Corinthians 6:2).

Testing the Spirits

This testing process, though brief, has yielded definitive results. We have tested five key doctrines of psychics against the Bible, and in each case, the psychics' teachings are completely at odds with the Bible. The psychics fail the test. The spirits who communicated these doctrines through psychics clearly are not of God but are rather demonic imposters intent on disseminating doctrines of demons (1 Timothy 4:1-3). These demonic imposters are headed by Satan, who is "a liar and the father of lies" (John 8:44). He is a master deceiver with thousands of years of experience. Tragically, the lies he and his demonic cohorts have embedded in the modern psychic movement are among the most deceptive ever and have led virtually tens of millions of Americans astray. The spiritual carnage is incalculable.

NINE

THE TRUTH ABOUT THE AFTERLIFE

P sychics teach—based on communications with spirits—that death is nothing to be feared. It simply involves a transition from physical life into the wonderful spirit world beyond—the Other Side.

Following death, people allegedly go through a tunnel into the light of God. Sylvia Browne claims, "I can't stress enough that there will never be a moment when you feel the least bit dead, or even unconscious, nor will your trip through the tunnel feel scary or unfamiliar."[1] Death is no big deal, according to psychics.

A Life Review

The Other Side, psychics say, has no judgment and no punishment. However, a life review will take place immediately after death in which people see how they affected other people positively or negatively:

> When someone passes over, they first attend a life review, during which they relive every single moment of their life, both the good and the bad. After this, many spirits feel a sense of regret over some of their actions or things that they said during their lifetime. So they want their loved ones to

know that they're sorry for what they did, that they love them, and that they're still around to support them.[2]

Psychics say that the dead often communicate such things when their living loved ones come in for a psychic reading. Taking care of unfinished business in this way costs the living between $300 and $750 per session.

A Multidimensional World

James Van Praagh believes heaven is a multidimensional world permeated by pure love, where spirits reside once they have departed from their physical bodies and before they take up new bodies through reincarnation.[3] He claims, "We live in a three-dimensional world. The spirit world is of the fourth, fifth, sixth, seventh dimensions. So, of course, we're limited with our three-dimensional laws here, with our vision and our feeling."[4]

Sylvia Browne is unique in her view that heaven exists three feet above ground level on earth, but it is at a much higher vibrational rate, so humans on earth typically do not perceive it. Her ability to perceive a wide range of vibrational frequencies, she claims, enables her to see what heaven is like.[5] She says the Other Side is a perfect mirror image of earth's natural topography but without erosion, pollution, or destruction.[6]

Browne makes this claim regarding our personal appearance:

All spirits on the Other Side are thirty years old, no matter what age they were when they died. They can assume their earthly appearance when they come to visit us, to make sure we recognize them; but going about their business on the Other Side, they can also choose their own physical attributes, from height to weight to hair color, and change any or all of those attributes whenever they like.[7]

Levels of Heaven

Psychics claim heaven has different levels, and people go to these different levels depending on how they lived their lives on earth. Those who excel in life and attain high spiritual awareness allegedly reside on a higher level in heaven, whereas lesser evolved souls reside on a lower level in heaven. People literally earn their destiny.

Van Praagh claims that some of the more advanced souls who exist in higher levels of heaven sometimes go to lower levels in order to assist those souls who lack spiritual awareness.[8] This sounds similar to the Hindu concept of the bodhisattva, in which a more advanced spiritual being turns back to help lesser-evolved beings.

Van Praagh also claims we will experience in the afterlife what we have dished out to others during earthly life. In other words, people experience a sense of heaven or hell according to the way they treated other people on earth.[9] If a person lives a decent life and gave out love, kindness, and compassion, that person will experience similar things in the afterlife, which is heaven. Those who did not love and were inconsiderate of other people will experience similar things in the afterlife, which can be much like hell.[10] Hell, we are told, is for those who need to reevaluate their lives.[11]

Char Margolis agrees, claiming that people who have not loved others but instead have harmed others will end up together on the Other Side, doing the same kinds of things to each other, thereby creating their own hell. Conversely, people who have expressed love and done good to other people will end up with others of the same kind, which will be truly heavenly. Margolis also claims, however, that wherever people end up after this lifetime, they can continually progress and evolve for the better through reincarnation. This means "we will continually be given opportunities to change, to try again, to make it better the next time."[12]

Everyone Welcome

Psychics claim that even pets go to the Other Side when they die, and they still visit us on earth whenever they want to. Your pet will allegedly "sit on the same chair, sleep in the same spot, and watch you very closely. It remembers the kindness and love it received from you on the earth, and it will often return to protect you."[13] Our pets "watch over us from there with the same pure, steadfast loyalty they gave during their lifetimes."[14]

Psychics assure us that in heaven there are beautiful temples, churches, and synagogues that share the countryside, with altars of every religion, all coexisting in peace and respect.

> Methodists and Buddhists happily and knowledgeably pray side by side at Judaic services, Catholics and Muslims are utterly comfortable singing hymns of praise with the Shinto monks, and the Baha'i. Joining to glorify God hand in hand is natural, necessary, and nurturing, as essential to our survival as the beating of our hearts.[15]

The School of Life

Psychic mediums believe earthly life is a school. As Van Praagh put it, "I think we've been here many, many times. I think we come back and learn lessons. I think this is our school room."[16]

Our education on earth utilizes the law of karma. In simplest form, this law states that people who do good things in this life build up good karma and will be born in a better condition in the next life. People who do bad things in this life will build up bad karma and will be born in a worse state in the next life. Van Praagh explains that "all our actions are repaid in kind, positively or negatively, in this life or another lifetime. The law of cause and effect is a natural, immutable law of the universe."[17] He suggests that what may appear to be an accident or even a natural disaster on earth is, in reality, not a chance occurrence. All things are based on karmic obligations. Everything happens for our own good. Everything happens for a purpose. "Your illness, or loss, or predicament is a part of your soul's growth."[18]

Psychics tell us that every time we incarnate into a new body, we decide when, where, and why. We choose to incarnate and come to earth in order to learn very specific lessons—to grow spiritually.[19] Before incarnating, Van Praagh claims, we discuss our soul's growth with a highly evolved group of beings known as the Etheric

Council. Through advice from these highly evolved beings, we choose the specific lessons we want to learn and the karmic debts we want to balance during the upcoming lifetime. Once we incarnate, our master guide—a spirit guide—makes sure we stay on track. "The Spirit Guide's job is to urge, nudge, encourage, advise, support, and, as their title suggests, guide us on our life's path."[20]

While Sylvia Browne does not make reference to an Etheric Council as Van Praagh does, she does refer to an Orientation team that aids individual souls as they make preparations for incarnating into bodies. "We gather in our Orientation room with our Spirit Guide, Orientation leader, and the rest of the Orientation team we've chosen, and with their help and the help of all the tools around us, based on our goals for our upcoming incarnation, we compose a chart, in incredible detail, for a life that will accomplish those goals."[21]

Browne claims we maintain tight control on various aspects of our incarnation. For example, she says, we choose our parents, our brothers and sisters, our physical appearance, the exact place, time, and date of birth, our friends, our spouses, our children, our bosses and coworkers, our pets, the neighborhoods we live in, the houses we live in, our skills and talents...even our flaws.[22] We even choose personal hardships we will encounter, as well as the time of our death. Everything is allegedly planned out on a chart in precise detail. Our spirit guides memorize our chart and supposedly always seek to keep us on the right track.

Immediately before we leave the Other Side to incarnate on earth, Browne claims, we have a personal meeting with the Messiah of our choice, whether Jesus, Buddha, Mohammed, or some other religious leader. They offer final spiritual counsel prior to our departure.[23]

Once we incarnate, we go through life living out what is contained on our chart, learning important lessons along the way. Once the process is complete and we die, we cross over to the Other Side yet again, where we eventually make preparations for yet another incarnation to learn even further lessons. On and on the process goes as we evolve to ever higher levels of spiritual attainment.

The Christian View

Psychics have constructed a rather elaborate theology of the afterlife. Frankly, I can see how a person who is not grounded in Christianity or in the Bible might fall for this theology and buy into it. I think this theology is one of Satan's cleverest inventions. It seeks to answer some ultimate questions: Why am I here? What is my purpose? What happens when I die? What is my ultimate goal?

Because this theology specifically makes light of death and communicates that all people cross over to the Other Side regardless of their religion (or lack thereof), people are drawn to this theology like bugs to a lantern. But like a bug flying into a lantern, the ultimate result is sudden destruction. Surely this is Satan's ultimate goal (John 8:44). He seeks to deceive people so that they go into eternity without Jesus Christ. Christians must therefore be ready to answer this bogus theology with truth from the Bible.

DEATH IS REAL AND FINAL

Death is real, and it is final. The New Testament word for death carries the idea of separation. At the moment of physical death, the Christian's spirit separates or departs from his or her body and goes to be with the Lord in heaven (2 Corinthians 5:8; Philippians 1:21). This is why, when Stephen was being put to death by stoning, he prayed, "Lord Jesus, receive my spirit" (Acts 7:59). At the moment of death "the spirit returns to God who gave it" (Ecclesiastes 12:7).

For the unbeliever, however, death holds grim prospects. At death the unbeliever's spirit departs from the body and goes not to heaven but to a place of great suffering and involuntarily confinement (Luke 16:19-31; 2 Peter 2:9).

The sobering reality is that death is final. Once people pass through death's door, they have no second chances. The unrighteous rich man in Luke 16:23-24 would have loved to have a second chance, but following the moment of death his destiny was eternally sealed. Hebrews 9:27 indicates that we live once, die once, and then face the judgment. For this reason the apostle Paul teaches that now is the day of salvation (2 Corinthians 6:2).

JUDGMENT FOLLOWS DEATH

Contrary to psychics' comforting teaching that all people will face a nonthreatening life review after death, Scripture indicates that all people—both Christians and non-Christians—will face God's judgment. More specifically, Christians will one day stand before the judgment seat of Christ (Romans 14:8-10). At that time Christ will examine each believer's life in regard to the things done while in the body. He will weigh the personal motives and intents of the heart.

The idea of a judgment seat comes from the athletic games of Paul's day. After the races and games concluded, the emperor himself often took his seat on an elevated throne, and one by one, the winning athletes came up to the throne to receive a reward. This reward was usually a wreath of leaves, a "victor's crown." Similarly, Christians will each stand before Christ the Judge and receive (or lose) rewards.

This judgment has nothing to do with whether or not the Christian will remain saved. Those who have placed faith in Christ are saved, and nothing threatens that. Believers are eternally secure in their salvation (Ephesians 4:30). This judgment rather has to do with the reception or loss of rewards.

The Christian's judgment will focus on his personal stewardship of the gifts, talents, opportunities, and responsibilities he received in this life. The very character of each Christian's life and service will be utterly laid bare under the unerring and omniscient vision of Christ, whose eyes are "like a flame of fire" (Revelation 1:14 NASB).

The Lord will judge each of our actions. The psalmist said to the Lord, "Surely you will reward each person according to what he has done" (Psalm 62:12; see also Matthew 16:27). In Ephesians

6:7-8 we read that the Lord "will reward everyone for whatever good he does, whether he is slave or free."

God will also scrutinize our thoughts. In Jeremiah 17:10 God said, "I the LORD search the heart and examine the mind, to reward a man according to his conduct, according to what his deeds deserve." The Lord "will bring to light what is hidden in darkness and will expose the motives of men's hearts" (1 Corinthians 4:5).

Finally, the scope of the believer's judgment will include all the words he has spoken. Christ once said that "men will have to give account on the day of judgment for every careless word they have spoken" (Matthew 12:35-37). If God records even our careless words, how much more will He take into account our calculated boastful claims, our cutting criticisms of others, our off-color jokes, and our unkind comments.

Unbelievers will also face God in judgment. The horrific judgment they face is the Great White Throne judgment, which leads to the lake of fire (Revelation 20:11-15). Christ is the divine Judge, and those who are judged are the unsaved dead of all time.

Those who face Christ at this judgment will be judged on the basis of their works (Revelation 20:12-13). It is critical to understand that they actually appear at this judgment because they are already unsaved. This judgment will not separate believers from unbelievers, for all who will experience it will have already made the choice during their lifetimes to reject God. Once they are before the divine Judge, they are judged according to their works not only to justify their condemnation but to determine the degree to which each person should be punished throughout eternity in hell.

HELL IS VERY REAL

Hell was not part of God's original creation, which He called good (Genesis 1:31). Hell was created later to accommodate the banishment of Satan and his fallen angels, who rebelled against God (Matthew 25:41). People who die rejecting Christ will join Satan and his fallen angels in this infernal place of suffering.

The Scriptures use a variety of words to describe the horrors of hell, including the lake of fire or of burning sulfur (Revelation

19:20; 20:14-15), the eternal fire (Matthew 25:41), the fiery furnace (Matthew 13:42), destruction (2 Thessalonians 1:8-9), and eternal punishment (Matthew 25:46). The greatest pain those in hell suffer is their permanent exclusion from God's presence. If ecstatic joy is found in God's presence (Psalm 16:11), then utter dismay is the result of the eternal absence of His presence. Any suggestion by psychics that hell is simply a stage some people briefly visit during their growth in progress in the afterlife is a huge deception.

God, of course, does not want to send anyone to hell. That's why He sent Jesus—to pay the penalty for our sins by dying on the cross (John 3:16-17). Unfortunately, not all people are willing to admit that they sin and to ask for forgiveness. They don't accept the payment of Jesus' death for them. God therefore lets them experience the results of their choice (Luke 16:19-31). C.S. Lewis once said that in the end there are two groups of people. One group of people says to God, "Thy will be done." These are those who have placed their faith in Jesus and will live forever with God in heaven. The second group of people are those to whom God says, sadly, "Thy will be done!" These are those who have rejected Jesus and will spend eternity apart from Him.

DEGREES OF PUNISHMENT IN HELL

Psychics often speak of different levels in heaven and even of hell, claiming that people end up on a particular level depending on how they treated others during their lives. *Heaven and hell have no such levels.* However, as we have seen, Christians will receive various degrees of reward in heaven, just as unbelievers will receive various degrees of punishment in hell.

Those who are eternally consigned to hell will experience a degree of punishment that is commensurate with the light they received. Luke 12:47-48 refers to degrees of punishment: "That servant who knows his master's will and does not get ready or does not do what his master wants will be beaten with many blows. But the one who does not know and does things deserving punishment will be beaten with few blows. From everyone who has been given much, much will be demanded; and from the one who has been entrusted with much, much more will be asked." Other relevant verses include Matthew 10:15; 16:27; Revelation 20:12-13; 22:12.

HEAVEN IS ONLY FOR BELIEVERS

Heaven is the splendorous eternal abode of the righteous—that is, those who have trusted in Christ for salvation and have therefore been made righteous by His atoning sacrifice. All who believe in Christ are heirs of the eternal kingdom (Galatians 3:29; 4:28-31; Titus 3:7; James 2:5). The righteousness of God that leads to life in heaven is available "through faith in Jesus Christ *to all those who believe*" (Romans 3:22). Jesus promised, "If anyone serves Me, let him follow Me; and where I am, there shall My servant also be" (John 12:26 NASB). Clearly, heaven is for believers in Jesus Christ, not for all people indiscriminately.

PEOPLE OF OTHER RELIGIONS ARE NOT SAVED

Contrary to the common claim of psychics that people of all religions (or no religion at all) are welcome in heaven, Scripture is clear that belief in a counterfeit God and a counterfeit gospel yields only a counterfeit salvation, which is no salvation at all. Christ's post-resurrection and pre-ascension commands to His disciples become a mockery if people of all religions are already saved. In Luke 24:47 (KJV) Christ commanded "that repentance and re-mission of sins should be preached *in his name* among all nations." Similarly, in Matthew 28:19 He said, "Therefore go and make disciples of all nations, baptizing them in the name of the Father and of the Son and of the Holy Spirit." These verses might well be stricken from the Scriptures if people without Christ are not lost. If people of different religions are not really lost, then the Lord's words were meaningless when He said to His disciples, "As the Father has sent me, I am sending you" (John 20:21). Why did the Father send Him? Jesus Himself explained that "the Son of Man came to seek and to save what was lost" (Luke 19:10).

If people of different religions do not need Christ and His salvation, then neither do we. Conversely, if we need Him, so do people of different religions. The Scriptures become a bundle of contradictions, the Savior becomes a false teacher, and the Christian message becomes "much ado about nothing" if people of different religions are not lost. A bold Peter said, "Salvation is found in no one else, for there is no other name under heaven given to men by which we must be saved" (Acts 4:12). The apostle Paul affirmed, "There is one God and one mediator between God and men, the man Christ Jesus" (1 Timothy 2:5). Jesus Himself asserted, "I am the way and the truth and the life. No one comes to the Father except through me" (John 14:6).

Other religions *do not* lead to God. The one sin for which God judged the people of Israel more severely than any other was that of participating in heathen religions. Again and again the Bible implies and states that God hates, despises, and utterly rejects anything associated with heathen religions and practices (for example, see Daniel 1:20; 2:2,10,27; 4:7; 5:7,11,15). Those who follow such idolatry are not groping their way to God—they have turned their backs on Him, following the ways of darkness.

LEARNING LESSONS IN LIFE?

Psychics teach that the reason human beings are reincarnated over and over again is to keep learning new lessons in each life. In a moment, we'll see that reincarnation is a false doctrine. For now, the point I want to make is that psychics without exception miss the one key lesson God wants all people to learn: All human beings are fallen in sin (Romans 3:23), cannot save themselves (Ephesians 2:8-9), and are therefore in dire need of salvation—a salvation found only by faith in Jesus Christ (John 3:16; Acts 16:31). Whoever dies before learning this one lesson errs eternally.

Scripture tells us that Satan blinds the minds of unbelievers (2 Corinthians 4:4). He does all he can to blind people to this one key lesson, filling their brains instead with psychic lies about the afterlife. The deception is enormous!

HUMANS NOT GODLIKE

Did you notice that human beings often come off looking very godlike in psychic theology? After all, in the afterlife, people get to choose all their physical features. And when it's time to reincarnate into another body, people choose their parents, their physical features, their neighborhoods, and everything else. In other words, people are basically gods who create their own realities.

Such is the height of human arrogance and folly. The reality is that man is a finite creature (Psalm 100:3), and because he is a creature, he does not compare with the one true, matchless God. No one on earth comes even remotely close to God's greatness and majesty. God Himself affirmed to Moses that He would do mighty miracles in Egypt "so that you may know that there is no one like Me in all the earth" (Exodus 9:14 NASB). Contrary to the prideful interpretation that man is godlike, creating his own reality, the recognition of creaturehood should lead to humility and worship of the one true God. "Come, let us bow down in worship, let us kneel before the LORD our Maker; for he is our God and we are the people of his pasture, the flock under his care" (Psalm 95:6-7). Scripture affirms that "God opposes the proud but gives grace to the humble" (James 4:6). We do well to follow Peter's advice to "humble yourselves, therefore, under God's mighty hand" (1 Peter 5:6).

REINCARNATION IS A FALSE DOCTRINE

Reincarnation is problematic on many levels.

Reincarnation is not fair. One must ask, why are people punished by means of karma for things they cannot remember having done in a previous life? And how do people become better by being punished for sins they do not remember? More pointedly, if young children develop cancer and die, what possible healing can be brought to their souls? They have no recollection of sins committed in a previous life, and even if they did have some such memory, they would not have the mental acumen to make sense of the hardship before they died. Where is the divine justice in this?

Reincarnation does not work. If the purpose of karma is to make human nature better, why have we not seen a noticeable improvement in human nature after all the millennia of reincarnations? Further, if reincarnation is so beneficial on a practical level, as psychics claim, how do they explain the immense and ever-worsening social and economic problems—including widespread poverty, starvation, disease, and horrible suffering—in India, where reincarnation has been systematically taught throughout its history? Still further, the philosophies of reincarnation and karma tend to make people passive toward social evil and injustice. In fact, belief in reincarnation serves as a strong motivation *not* to be a good neighbor and lend a helping hand. After all, people in pain must be suffering because they have not yet paid off the prescribed karmic debt for the sins they committed in a previous life. If we help suffering people, we will only guarantee they will be born in a worse state in the next life to pay off the karmic debt they were supposed to pay off in the present life. Further, we would also accumulate more bad karmic debt for interfering with the law of karma. Reincarnation creates a no-win scenario.

Reincarnation is fatalistic. The law of karma guarantees that whatever we sow in the present life, we will invariably reap in the next life. If we sow good seeds in the present life, we will reap a nice harvest (have a better situation) in the next life. If we sow bad seeds in the present life, we will reap a bad harvest (have a worse situation) in the next life. Nothing we can do will alter this chain of events. It works infallibly and inexorably. This also means that whatever sufferings we may face in the present life are guaranteed to be part of our lives because of what we did in our past lives. Such a fatalistic philosophy can lead to despair.

Reincarnation is contrary to the Bible. Scripture indicates that each person lives once as a mortal on earth, dies once, and then faces judgment (Hebrews 9:27). We do not get a second chance by reincarnating into another body. Scripture indicates that at death believers in the Lord Jesus go to heaven (2 Corinthians 5:8) while unbelievers go to a place of punishment (Luke 16:19-31). Moreover, Jesus taught that people decide their eternal destiny in a single lifetime (Matthew 25:46). This is precisely why the apostle Paul emphasized that "now is the day of salvation" (2 Corinthians 6:2).

Further, reincarnationists grossly underestimate the seriousness of the sin problem (Matthew 9:12; 12:34; 15:14; 23:16-26; Mark

1:15; 7:20-23; Luke 11:13,42-52; 15:10; 19:10; John 3:19-21; 8:34; 12:35-46). Indeed, the reincarnational belief that man can solve his own sin problem with a little help from karma (throughout many lifetimes) is itself a manifestation of the blindness that is part and parcel of human sin. Our problem is so severe that we need outside help—the help of a divine Savior. We do not need a mere karmic tune-up; we need a brand new engine (new life from Jesus—John 3:1-5).

The doctrine of reincarnation simply isn't true, and because reincarnation is the backbone of psychic theology, psychic theology is utterly untenable and misleading. How tragic that countless people around the world—even some who claim to be Christians—have swallowed the lie of reincarnation.

Psychics teach that death is no big deal and happens regularly throughout one's spiritual journey through innumerable lifetimes (by means of reincarnation), but Christianity teaches that humans live once, die once, and then face the judgment. Psychics teach that humans face a nonthreatening life review following death, but Christianity teaches that all humans will face a judgment by God Himself, and woe unto any who—having failed to trust in Christ during earthly life—must face God at the Great White Throne judgment. Psychics teach that hell is just a temporary place of learning for those who didn't do well in earthly life, but Christianity teaches it is the eternal abode of those who reject Christ. Psychics teach that people of all religions go to heaven, but Christianity teaches that only those who trust in Christ for salvation go to heaven. In short, psychics—based on their communications with spirits (who, as we have seen, cannot be dead people and therefore must be demonic)—promote a theology of the afterlife strategically designed to lead millions astray. Ultimately, then, psychic theology is a theology of damnation and eternal perdition.

TEN

SHARPENING DISCERNMENT ON PSYCHIC MEDIUMS

We have considered the methodology psychics use when they do readings, concluding that in many cases they fish for information. At other times they cheat by deriving information beforehand, and sometimes they are in genuine contact with demonic spirits. We have also noted psychics' dismal accuracy rate and have probed some of their common excuses for misses. Then we "tested the spirits," proving that the true source of psychic doctrines is not God but rather evil spirits intent on deceiving humankind. Finally, we contrasted the psychics' view of the afterlife with that of Christianity.

In this final chapter, we will add some finishing touches to our biblical discernment of psychic mediums. Let's not forget Solomon's exhortation in Proverbs 3:21: "Preserve sound judgment and discernment, do not let them out of your sight." We are not to let them out of our sight because they will guard our minds from all kinds of deception—including the deception being disseminated on a massive level by modern psychic mediums.

Occultism Condemned

Some psychic mediums claim they have a gift from God, but the Bible condemns all forms of occultism, divination, and sorcery. Leviticus 19:26 commands, "Do not practice divination or sorcery." Leviticus 19:31 instructs, "Do not turn to mediums or seek out spiritists, for you will be defiled by them. I am the LORD your God." The Old Testament is clear that a person who consorts with familiar spirits is cursed by God (Leviticus 19:31; 20:6). Exodus 22:18 commands that sorceresses are to be put to death. We read in Leviticus 20:27, "A man or woman who is a medium or spiritist among you must be put to death. You are to stone them; their blood will be on their own heads."

Second Kings 21:6 tells us that Manasseh "consulted mediums and spiritists. He did much evil in the eyes of the LORD, provoking him to anger." By contrast, "Josiah got rid of the mediums and spiritists, the household gods, the idols and all the other detestable things seen in Judah and Jerusalem. This he did to fulfill the requirements of the law written in the book that Hilkiah the priest had discovered in the temple of the LORD" (2 Kings 23:24).

In 1 Samuel 28:3, Saul "expelled the mediums and spiritists from the land." Later, however, we read that "Saul died because he was unfaithful to the LORD; he did not keep the word of the LORD and even consulted a medium for guidance" (1 Chronicles 10:13).

Acts 19:19 reveals that many who converted to Christ in Ephesus destroyed all the paraphernalia they formerly used for occultism and divination: "A number who had practiced sorcery brought their scrolls together and burned them publicly. When they calculated the value of the scrolls, the total came to fifty thousand drachmas." (A drachma was about a day's wages.)

In the Bible, God categorically condemns all spiritistic activities as heinous sins against Him. Deuteronomy 18:10-11 is clear: "Let no one be found among you...who is a medium or spiritist or who consults the dead. Anyone who does these things is detestable to the LORD." Let's be clear: This means that the spiritistic practices of James Van Praagh, John Edward, Sylvia Browne, Char Margolis, and all other modern psychics are detestable (literally, an abomination) to the Lord.

Scholar Stafford Wright, in his book *Christianity and the*

Occult, examined all such Old Testament passages on spiritism. This is his conclusion: "It is beyond doubt that the Old Testament bans any attempt to contact the departed. This is true of the law, the historical books, and the prophets. Is there the slightest sign that the New Testament lifts the ban?"[1]

Dead Humans Are Not Available for Psychic Contact

Earlier in the book, in our critique of ghost phenomena (chapter 5), we saw that people are unavailable to make appearances on earth as ghosts. Similarly, human beings are unavailable for contact by psychics.

At death, the believer's spirit departs from the physical body and immediately goes into the Lord's presence in heaven (2 Corinthians 5:8; Philippians 1:21-23). The unbeliever's spirit departs from the body, goes to a place of great suffering, and is involuntarily confined until the future day of judgment (Luke 16:19-31; 2 Peter 2:9). The point is that departed people, whether believers or unbelievers, are confined in their respective domains, and God prohibits contact between earth and these domains (Deuteronomy 18:10-11).

The story of the rich man and Lazarus in Luke 16:19-31 illustrates this for us. The rich man and Lazarus had died and gone into the afterlife. The rich man—an unbeliever—was suffering great agony. He wanted to contact his living brothers to warn them. However, he was not permitted to do so. Communication between the dead and the living was simply not permitted (Deuteronomy 18:10-11). Since this is the case, we can surmise that if a psychic is encountering any spirit entity at all, it is a demonic spirit and not a dead human (see 1 Timothy 4:1-3; 1 John 4:1).

What about the Medium of Endor?

Psychics and spiritists sometimes claim support for their practices from the pages of the Bible. They often refer to King Saul's experience with the medium at Endor as a proof that spiritism is acceptable (1 Samuel 28).

The biblical account of the medium at Endor is quite controversial, and Christians have expressed different views. A minority believe the medium worked a miracle by demonic powers and actually brought Samuel back from the dead. In support of this view, certain passages seem to indicate that demons have the power to perform lying signs and wonders (Matthew 7:22; 2 Corinthians 11:14; 2 Thessalonians 2:9-10; Revelation 16:14). This view is unlikely, however, because Scripture also reveals that death is final (Hebrews 9:27), the dead cannot return (2 Samuel 12:23; Luke 16:24-27), and demons cannot usurp or overpower God's authority over life and death (Job 1:10-12).

A second view is that the medium did not really bring up Samuel from the dead, but a demonic spirit simply impersonated the prophet. Those who hold to this view note that certain verses indicate that demons can deceive people who try to contact the dead (Leviticus 19:31; Deuteronomy 18:11; 1 Chronicles 10:13). This view is unlikely, however, because the passage affirms that Samuel did in fact return from the dead, that he provided a prophecy that actually came to pass, and that demons would not have been likely to utter God's truth because the devil is the father of lies (John 8:44).

A third view is that God sovereignly and miraculously allowed Samuel's spirit to appear in order to rebuke Saul for his sin. Samuel's spirit did not appear as a result of the medium's powers (for indeed, no human has the power to summon dead humans—Luke 16:24-27; Hebrews 9:27) but only because God sovereignly brought it about. This view is supported by the fact that Samuel actually returned from the dead (1 Samuel 28:14), and this caused the medium to shriek with fear (see verse 12). The medium's cry of astonishment indicates that this appearance of Samuel was not the result of her usual tricks.

Though God allowed Samuel's spirit to appear on this one occasion, we should not take this to mean that mediums have any real power to summon the dead. God had a one-time purpose for this one-time special occasion. This passage is therefore *descriptive*, not *prescriptive*. That is, it simply describes something that happened historically. It does not prescribe something that people should expect in the future.

Satan Can Masquerade as Dead People

Earlier in the book, in my critique of ghosts and hauntings (chapter 5), we saw that since Satan can masquerade as an angel of light (2 Corinthians 11:14), he surely also has the ability to masquerade as a dead person haunting a house as a ghost. Likewise, he surely has the ability to masquerade as a dead person who communicates with a psychic medium. He is a masterful counterfeiter. We have seen that he has his own church, gospel, and prophets.

Likewise, we have good reason to suspect that Satan counterfeits dead humans to deceive the living through psychics like James Van Praagh, Sylvia Browne, John Edward, and Char Margolis. Demons are more than willing to masquerade as dead humans to deceive tens of millions of people and draw them away from Jesus Christ.

The Test of Deuteronomy 13:1-3

Because psychics and demonic spirits can be so deceptive, Scripture has given us an extremely important test to use. Deuteronomy 13:1-3 says that if a "sign or wonder" comes to pass from a prophet or a "dreamer of dreams," and what they said comes true, but then that prophet or dreamer asks that we follow other gods, we are not to listen to what this person says. This means that if a psychic gives a correct prediction about some event but then contradicts God's Word in his or her teachings, then what he or she says cannot be from God, and we must reject it.

A survey of psychic teachings proves that they fail the test of Deuteronomy 13:1-3, for they hold to an unbiblical view of God. Some hold to a pantheistic view of God ("all is God"). Some hold that God is a mere impersonal force or "infinite intelligence." Some hold that God is a "divine spark" that is within all human beings. Some recognize God the Father but also God the Mother. Aside from an unbiblical view of God, psychics without exception have an unbiblical view of Jesus, sin, salvation, and the afterlife (see chapter 8). Clearly, then, even if a modern psychic should stumble onto a correct prediction that actually comes to pass, we should nevertheless reject that psychic's teaching because he or she sets forth unbiblical doctrines.

No Innate Psychic Powers

Contrary to the claims of many psychics, human beings do not possess an innate psychic ability. Acts 16:16-19 proves that spiritists and psychics are always connected to a demonic spirit being. In this passage, we find an account of a slave girl who had a spirit of divination. When the apostle Paul cast this spirit out of the girl, she lost all her psychic powers. If she possessed innate psychic powers, her powers would not have vanished when Paul cast the spirit out. The same is true with all modern psychics today. They have no innate powers as they claim they do, but rather they are in contact with demonic spirits who energize any psychic abilities they may have.

Psychics are also incorrect in their claim that the biblical prophets possessed innate power. In every case, God gave the prophets direct revelation to speak to the people. That's why prophets often prefaced their revelation with the words, "Thus saith the LORD" (for example, Ezekiel 21:9 KJV). The prophets never initiated the revelations they received from God, nor did they initiate visions. Rather, the Lord always chose His prophets and gave them direct special revelation to speak. God *moved*, and the prophets *mouthed* God's truths.

A Former Psychic's Assessment

Contrary to what psychics may claim, they are playing with fire when they contact spirit entities. Even psychics and spiritists themselves acknowledge evil spirit entities or "evil energies." That's why they try to take steps to protect themselves.

Marcia Montenegro is a former psychic and occultist who is now a Christian. From her many years of involvement in occultism, she recalls the dangers:

> As this writer's psychic abilities expanded, so did the frightening experiences. Many of this writer's friends and associates in the occult often had similar experiences. In fact, it is common practice for a psychic to call on benevolent protective forces or to visualize "white light" (supposedly for protection) before practicing a psychic technique, doing a reading or spirit contact. What do they think they are protecting themselves from? By doing this, the psychics acknowledge the existence of evil or harmful beings, but how do they know these beings are not disguising themselves as benevolent spirits or guides? What law says a white light is a barrier to evil entities? Why would such a light keep out any spirits? Maybe the evil entities have been laughing all these years at this flimsy "protection" as they fed false information to the psychics and pretended to be helpful.[2]

I think Marcia is right on target. Psychics are being duped by these evil spirits, who have been duping people for thousands of years and know how to put on a good disguise. These spirits mimic our dead loved ones, and their goal is to lead the living to believe that they need not fear death, that death is a simple transition, that all people—regardless of what religion they subscribe to—cross over into the Other Side, and that they need not trust in Christ for the joys of heaven. Make no mistake about it, the powers of darkness hate Jesus Christ with a seething hatred, and they will do anything they can to deceive people away from believing in Him.

Police and Psychics

Sometimes I hear people say that if the police and FBI utilize the services of psychics, then psychics must be accurate. However, this is an unwise conclusion. Former chief hostage negotiator for the FBI Clint Van Zandt has noted—based on many years of experience—that the information that typically comes from psychics regarding crimes is very vague. They often say something like "You will find the body near a large body of water." This nonspecific kind of information is not helpful. Van Zandt says he's not aware of any cases that have been solved solely on the basis of information provided by a psychic.[3]

In most cases, the police don't seek out psychics. Rather, the families of victims ask the police to consider consulting a psychic, and the police often oblige for the family's sake. Because so many families believe in psychic phenomena today, police are bound to be asked quite often to consult psychics in an effort to solve crimes.

Trances and Altered States

Psychic mediums often go into an altered state of consciousness when opening themselves up to spirits on the Other Side. Researchers have noted that altered states of consciousness can lead to harmful consequences. Indeed, Christian scholar Kenneth Boa documents an increasing number of reports regarding people who have been harmed by such altered states.[4]

Leon Otis of Stanford Research Institute has documented that some who attain an altered state of consciousness develop increased anxiety, confusion, and depression.[5] The severity of these symptoms was directly correlated with the length of time the person was in an altered state.[6] Researcher Gary Schwartz likewise found that too much deep meditation—leading to an altered state—can hinder logical thought processes.[7] Researcher Arnold Ludwig found that "as a person enters or is in an ASC [altered state of consciousness], he often experiences fear of losing his grip on reality, and losing his self-control."[8] These facts alone ought to be enough to dissuade people from wanting to increase their psychic skills, as today's primetime psychics encourage them to do in their books.

Exploiting the Bereaved

I echo the sentiment of many that today's psychics are preying upon the vulnerability of the bereaved.[9] Almost every person in the United States has experienced the pain of losing a loved one in death. This single fact is what accounts for the huge popularity of psychics: They claim to be able to make contact with these dead loved ones, and they do so for between $300 and $750 per session. Sadly, people care about their dead loved ones so much that no expense is too much. Psychics know this, and even though they claim they are doing what they do because they want to help people, help that costs up to $750 for a half hour seems disingenuous at best.

POSTSCRIPT

We've taken quite a journey in this book. We've examined the occultic world of psychics, mediums, ghosts, and the paranormal. In the process, we've taken a hard look at today's hottest primetime psychics—James Van Praagh, John Edward, Sylvia Browne, and Char Margolis. We've also examined their methods, their teachings, and their rate of accuracy.

We have devoted out heaviest attention to providing a Christian assessment of such phenomena. This assessment is engineered to equip Christians of all ages—teenagers, college students, and adults—to think biblically about these issues.

You will recall from chapter 1 that current statistics indicate that some 73 percent of our nation's teenagers have participated in psychic phenomena. Seven million of them claim they've encountered a spirit entity, and two million of them claim to even have psychic powers. We also found that among churchgoing teenagers, only 28 percent say they've been taught anything at church to help shape their views of the supernatural world. We further found that a high percentage of college students as well as college professors believe in paranormal phenomena. Among adults in our country, some 38 percent—over one third of all Americans—believe that the spirits of dead humans can come back to visit us.[1] Tragically, from my personal experience, I can attest that many Christians have been contaminated by paranormal ideas.

While writing this book, I spoke at a church about the dangers of involvement in psychic phenomena. After the church service, I learned that a relatively young man at the church had recently lost his wife to cancer. He told other Christians at the church that he was intending to consult a medium so he could communicate with his dead wife. What a sad illustration this is of the lack of discernment in Christian churches today!

I noted earlier in the book that many Christians may consult with a psychic medium because they believe that such psychics are Christians. Recall that Sylvia Browne often refers to God, Christ, and the Holy Spirit during her television appearances and claims to do all that she does by the grace of God.[2] Likewise, psychic John Edward claims to be a Catholic and even prays the rosary before each and every psychic reading. Char Margolis claims her psychic ability is God-given. The danger is that many Christians who are undiscerning—and who lack a thorough Bible knowledge—may believe such psychics who say they are Christians, and those Christians may feel free to utilize their services. They may have virtually no idea that by so doing, they are committing an abomination before God (Deuteronomy 18:10-12).

More than ever, Christians in this country need discernment about mediums, ghosts, and psychic phenomena. My hope and prayer is that this book has helped meet that need.

As I close, I invite you to visit my website at www.ronrhodes. org. At this site, you will find a link titled "The Truth Behind Mediums, Ghosts, and Psychic Phenomena." By clicking on this link, you'll find a full listing of articles written by recognized Christian authorities on this issue. This is provided so that you can do further study on this subject in an easy, convenient way.

May the Lord bless you and keep you!

NOTES

CLOSE ENCOUNTERS WITH THE OTHER SIDE

1. For example, see Leslie Rule, *Ghosts Among Us: True Stories of Spirit Encounters* (Kansas City: Andrews McMeel Publishing, 2004), p. 14; Hazel Denning, *Hauntings: Real-Life Encounters with Troubled Spirits* (New York: Barnes & Noble, 2000), pp. 13-14; USA Weekend Editors, *I Never Believed in Ghosts Until...* (Chicago: Contemporary Books, 1992), pp. 180-81.

CHAPTER 1—PARANORMAL: THE NEW NORMAL?

1. Pauline Chiou, "Listening to the Voices of Ghosts," CBS News, February 3, 2006.

2. Marcia Montenegro, "I See Dead People," *Christian Research Journal*, vol. 25, no. 1, 2003, Internet edition.

3. Cited in John Ankerberg and John Weldon, *Cult Watch* (Eugene: Harvest House Publishers, 1991), p. 249, insert added.

4. *The O'Reilly Factor*, May 13, 1999.

5. Montenegro, *"I See Dead People."*

6. Brian Farha, "Well, Larry—You've Done It Again," *Skeptical Inquirer*, November 1, 2004, Internet edition.

7. Daniel Taverne, "Trends Acknowledge Psychic Abilities," *The American Chronicle*, January 10, 2006, Internet edition.

8. Roxana Hadadi, "Do You Believe In Ghosts?" *Diamondback Online News*, February 3, 2006, Internet edition.

9. *Wikipedia*, s.v. "Parapsychology."

10. David Kinnaman, "New Research Explores Teenage Views and Behavior Regarding the Supernatural," *The Barn Update*, January 23, 2006, Internet edition.

11. Ibid.

12. Alex Vickroth, "Hunting B'more Ghosts," The *Johns Hopkins Newsletter*, December 2, 2005, Internet edition.

13. William Keck, "Lots of Life in 'Ghost Whisperer,'" *USA Today*, February 1, 2006, Internet edition.

14. Ibid.

15. Kimberly Speight, "Creator of Ghost Whisperer Touched by Supernatural," *Chicago Sun-Times*, December 30, 2005, Internet edition.

16. Ibid.

17. Ibid.

18. Robert Dominguez, "Ghost World," *New York Daily News,* August 21, 2005, Internet edition.

19. Ibid.

20. Dan Burns, "Ghost Hunter Searches for the Paranormal," *LocalSource.com,* December 22, 2005, Internet edition.

21. Michael Acker and Miguel Juarez, "Local Ghost Hunter Stars in TLC Reality Series," *Tri-Town News,* December 8, 2005, Internet edition.

22. Stacy Shaikin, "Ghost Trackers," *Calgary Sun,* December 24, 2005, Internet edition.

23. Dominguez, "Ghost World."

24. Cited in "What's New in the Headlines," *Christian Research Newsletter,* January/February 1991, p. 3.

25. Sylvia Browne, *Life on the Other Side* (New York: Signet, 2000), p. 6.

26. Don Kaplan, "Bring Us Your Dead," *New York Post,* December 14, 2001, Internet edition.

27. Bill Hoffmann, "Psychic Reunites Sonny & Cher," *New York Post,* April 30, 1998, Internet edition.

28. Peter Carlin, "Maximum Medium," *People Weekly,* March 9, 1998, Internet edition.

29. Richard Abanes, *Cults, New Religious Movements, and Your Family* (Wheaton: Crossway Books, 1998), p. 39.

30. "Jimmy Carter's Psychic Connection," *NewsMax.com,* January 1, 2006, Internet edition.

31. J.D. Prose, "Community Colleges Offer Unusual Courses," *Beaver County Times,* January 30, 2006, Internet edition.

32. "Boo! Britain Gets First Ghost School," *CHINAdaily,* January 21, 2006, Internet edition.

33. "Free Email Course on How to Develop Your Intuition," PR Newswire, December 9, 2005, Internet edition.

34. Andre Salvail, "Ghost Seminar Draws from Across the U.S.," *Aspen Daily News,* November 19, 2005, Internet edition.

35. Scott Jason, "Hundreds Gather for Psychic Readings," *Chico Enterprise Record,* November 13, 2005, Internet edition.

36. Misty Maynard, "Paranormal Weekend Materializes," *Maysville Online.com,* January 19, 2006, Internet edition.

37. Stephen Wagner, "The Scariest Games," *About.com,* October 2005, Internet edition.

38. "Radio Show Focuses on the Paranormal," TwinCities.com, January 1, 2006, Internet edition.

39. Press release on I-Newswire, November 3, 2005, Internet edition.

40. Leslie Rule, *Ghosts Among Us* (Kansas City: Andrews McMeel Publishing, 2004), p. 174.

41. "9/11 Victims Speak Out in New Book," PRWeb, January 6, 2006, Internet edition.

CHAPTER 2—UNDERSTANDING THE APPEAL

1. John Ankerberg and John Weldon, *Cult Watch* (Eugene: Harvest House Publishers, 1991), p. 267.

2. Cathy Hainer, "Lessons for Living Are Heaven-Sent," *USA Today,* March 19, 1998, Internet edition.

3. James Van Praagh, *Talking to Heaven* (New York: Signet, 1997), p. 24.

4. Ibid., p. 25.

5. Ibid., p. 30.

6. Hainer, "Lessons for Living Are Heaven-Sent."

7. Van Praagh, *Talking to Heaven,* p. 29.

8. Sylvia Browne, *Life on the Other Side* (New York: Signet, 2000), p. 34.

9. Ibid., p. 35.

10. Ibid.

11. Retta Blaney, "A Psychic Guru Prays the Rosary," *National Catholic Reporter,* February 3, 2006, Internet edition.

12. Char Margolis website.

13. Sylvia Browne website.

14. Orville Swenson, *The Perilous Path of Occultism* (Canada: Briercrest Books, 1987), p. 14.

15. Chris Ballard, "John Edward is the Oprah of the Other Side," *New York Times Magazine,* July 29, 2001, Internet edition.

16. Ibid.

17. Randy Alcorn, *Heaven* (Wheaton: Tyndale, 2004), p. xxi.

18. Browne, *Life on the Other Side,* p. 2.

19. Walter Martin, *The Kingdom of the Cults* (Minneapolis: Bethany House Publishers, 2003), p. 264.

20. James Van Praagh, *Heaven and Earth* (New York: Pocket Books, 2001), p. 77.

21. The Barna Group, "New Research Explores Teenage Views and Behavior Regarding the Supernatural," January 23, 2006, Internet edition.

22. Ibid.

23. Daniel Tavern, "Psychic: More than Myth," *The American Chronicle,* November 28, 2005, Internet edition.

24. Van Praagh, *Talking to Heaven,* p. 5.

25. Van Praagh, *Heaven and Earth,* p. 27.

26. Review of *Talking to Heaven* by James Van Praagh, *Publishers Weekly,* October 27, 1999, Internet edition.

27. Char Margolis website.

28. Char Margolis, *Questions from Earth, Answers from Heaven* (New York: St. Martin's, 2000), p. 26.

29. Char Margolis, on *The O'Reilly Factor,* May 13, 1999.

CHAPTER 3—A PRIMER ON PSYCHIC PHENOMENA

1. Ron Enroth, "The Occult," *Evangelical Dictionary of Theology,* ed. Walter Elwell (Grand Rapids: Baker, 1984), p. 787.

2. James Van Praagh, *Heaven and Earth* (New York: Pocket Books, 2001), p. 78.

3. John Edward, *One Last Time* (New York: Berkley Books, 1999), p. 53.

4. Sylvia Browne, *Life on the Other Side* (New York: Signet, 2000), p. 3.

5. James Van Praagh, *Talking to Heaven* (New York: Signet, 1997), p. 46.

6. Ibid., p. 49.

7. Ibid., p. 51.

8. "An Interview with Psychic and Medium James Van Praagh," *Mysteries Magazine,* January 1, 2005, Internet edition.

9. Sylvia Browne with Lindsay Harrison, *Phenomenon* (New York: Dutton, 2005), p. 179.

10. Elliot Miller, *A Crash Course on the New Age Movement* (Grand Rapids: Baker, 1990), p. 141.

11. Browne, *Phenomenon,* p. 60.

12. John Ankerberg and John Weldon, *Cult Watch* (Eugene: Harvest House Publishers, 1991), p. 174.

13. Ibid.

14. Char Margolis, *Questions from Earth, Answers from Heaven* (New York: St. Martin's, 2000), p. 196.

15. Kenneth Boa, *Cults, World Religions, and You* (Wheaton: Victor Books, 1986), p. 132.

16. Jon Klimo, *Channeling* (Los Angeles: Tarcher, 1987), chapter 2.

17. Hazel Denning, *Hauntings* (New York: Barnes & Noble, 2000), p. 209.

18. Browne, *Phenomenon,* p. 266.

19. Van Praagh, *Talking to Heaven,* p. 63.

20. Boa, *Cults, World Religions, and You,* p. 132.

21. Van Praagh, *Heaven and Earth,* pp. 93-94.

22. Browne, *Phenomenon,* p. 67.

23. Van Praagh, *Talking to Heaven,* p. 49.

24. Browne, *Phenomenon,* p. 66.

25. Van Praagh, *Talking to Heaven,* p. 50.

26. George Mather and Larry Nichols, *Dictionary of Cults, Sects, Religions and the Occult* (Grand Rapids: Zondervan, 1993), p. 86.

27. Denning, *Hauntings*, p. 205.

28. *Columbia Encyclopedia* s.v. "Spiritism."

29. Browne, *Phenomenon*, p. 29.

30. *Wikipedia*, s.v. "Ghost."

31. Browne, *Phenomenon*, p. 124.

32. John Ankerberg and John Weldon, "What Is the Historic Connection Between Halloween and Ghosts?" Ankerberg Theological Institute website.

33. Van Praagh, *Heaven and Earth*, p. 242.

34. Van Praagh, *Talking to Heaven*, p. 94.

35. Van Praagh, *Heaven and Earth*, p. 100.

36. Kurt Koch, *Between Christ and Satan* (Grand Rapids: Kregel, 1972), p. 112.

37. Van Praagh, *Heaven and Earth*, p. 103.

38. Koch, *Between Christ and Satan*, p. 107.

39. Van Praagh, *Heaven and Earth*, p. 103.

40. Ibid., p. 101.

CHAPTER 4—ALLEGED GHOSTS AND HAUNTINGS

1. Sylvia Browne, *The Other Side and Back* (New York: Signet, 2000), p. 160.

2. Sylvia Browne, *Life on the Other Side* (New York: Signet, 2000), p. 56.

3. Leslie Rule, *Coast to Coast Ghosts* (Kansas City: Andrews McMeel Publishing, 2001), p. 92.

4. Browne, *Life on the Other Side*, p. 56.

5. Browne, *The Other Side and Back*, p. 160.

6. Ibid., pp. 149-50.

7. *Wikipedia*, s.v. "Ghost."

8. Robbi Courtaway, "Spirits Don't Frighten This Woman," *Kirkwood-Webster Journal*, November 30, 2005, Internet edition.

9. Hazel Denning, *Hauntings* (New York: Barnes & Noble, 2000), p. 3.

10. Char Margolis, *Questions from Earth, Answers from Heaven* (New York: St. Martin's, 2000), pp. 178-79.

11. James Van Praagh, *Heaven and Earth* (New York: Pocket Books, 2001), p. 242.

12. Jamie Swift, "Ghost Hunters on the Prowl," *King County Journal*, October 12, 2005, Internet edition.

13. *Wikipedia*, s.v. "Ghost."

14. Ibid.

15. Stefanie Scarlett, "Area Woman Pens Tales of Girlhood Ghosts," *Fort Wayne Journal Gazette*, January 14, 2006, Internet edition.

16. Rule, *Coast to Coast Ghosts*, p. 92.
17. Ibid.
18. Nancy Roberts, *Haunted Houses* (Guilford: Globe Pequot Press, 1998), n.p.
19. Rule, *Coast to Coast Ghosts*, p. 11.
20. Van Praagh, *Heaven and Earth*, p. 91.
21. Alex Vickroth, "Hunting B'more Ghosts," *The Johns Hopkins Newsletter*, December 2, 2005, Internet edition.
22. Edward Eveld, "Ghost Hunting?" *Knight Ridder Newspapers*, November 17, 2005, Internet edition.
23. Van Praagh, *Heaven and Earth*, p. 90.
24. Rule, *Coast to Coast Ghosts*, p. 103.
25. Leslie Rule, *Ghosts Among Us* (Kansas City: Andrews McMeel Publishing, 2004), p. xv.
26. Another theory circulating today is that poltergeists are not ghosts at all, but rather phenomena caused by the minds of troubled adolescents. Without realizing what they're doing, these youths allegedly affect the environment and cause various disturbances with mind-over-matter energy.
27. John Ankerberg and John Weldon, "What Is the Historic Connection Between Halloween and Ghosts?" Ankerberg Theological Institute website.
28. Rule, *Coast to Coast Ghosts*, p. 40.
29. Sylvia Browne, *Phenomenon* (New York: Dutton, 2005), p. 138.
30. Denning, *Hauntings*, pp. 13-14.
31. *I Never Believed in Ghosts Until...* (Chicago: Contemporary Books, 1992), pp. 180-81.
32. Vickroth, "Hunting B'more Ghosts."
33. Ray Routhier, "On the Trail of Ghosts," *Portland Press Herald*, October 30, 2005, Internet edition.
34. Jay Rath, "Paranormal: Beyond the Range of Normal Experience or Scientific Explanation?" *Wisconsin State Journal*, October 31, 2004, Internet edition.
35. Ibid.
36. Ibid.
37. Andrea Hawn, "Finding Out for Herself: Vienna Woman Researches the Paranormal," *The Southern*, November 11, 2005, Internet edition.
38. Edward Eveld, "Ghost Hunting? It Helps to Know Where to Go," *Knight Ridder Newspapers*, November 17, 2005, Internet edition.
39. Van Praagh, *Talking to Heaven*, p. 95.
40. Rule, *Coast to Coast Ghosts*, p. 138.
41. Ibid., p. 194.
42. Browne, *Life on the Other Side*, p. 60.
43. Ibid., p. 61.

CHAPTER 5—THE TRUTH ABOUT GHOSTS AND HAUNTINGS

1. Meryl Corant, "Hunting for the Paranormal," November 13, 2005 report on WHSV TV, Internet edition.

2. *Wikipedia*, s.v. "Ghost."

3. Gilliam Bennett, "Seeing Ghosts: Experiences of the Paranormal," *Folklore*, December 1, 2004, Internet edition.

4. Cited in Michael Shermer, "Perspective on Space Aliens—We See What We Believe We See," *Los Angeles Times*, June 26, 1997, p. B-9.

5. Ray Routhier, "On the Trail of Ghosts," *Portland (MA) Press Herald*, October 30, 2005, Internet edition.

6. Byron Crawford, "Paranormal Pranks on Fisherville Family Left Them Spell-bound," *Louisville Courier-Journal*, October 30, 2005, Internet edition.

7. Glenn Sparks, "Paranormal Depictions in the Media: How Do They Affect What People Believe?" *Skeptical Inquirer*, July 1, 1998, Internet edition.

8. John Ankerberg and John Weldon, "What Is the Historic Connection Between Halloween and Ghosts?" Ankerberg Theological Institute website.

9. Kurt Koch, *Christian Counseling and Occultism* (Grand Rapids: Kregel, 1972), pp. 184-85, 188.

10. Char Margolis, *Questions from Earth, Answers from Heaven* (New York: St. Martin's, 2000), pp. 34-35.

11. Leslie Rule, *Coast to Coast Ghosts* (Kansas City: Andrews McMeel Publishing, 2001), p. 195.

12. John Ankerberg and John Weldon, *Cult Watch* (Eugene: Harvest House Publishers, 1991), p. 176.

CHAPTER 6—HOW PSYCHIC MEDIUMS OPERATE

1. Kevin Todeschi, "James Van Praagh—Exploring the Other Side," *Venture Inward*, June 1, 2005, Internet edition.

2. James Van Praagh, *Talking to Heaven* (New York: Signet, 1997), p. 193.

3. Van Praagh, *Talking to Heaven*, p. 111.

4. Stephanie Schorow, "Spirited Discussion," *The Boston Herald*, May 11, 1998, Internet edition.

5. Dru Sefton, "Van Praagh: Steering the Mediumship," *Kansas City Star*, May 17, 1998, Internet edition.

6. John Edward, *After Life* (New York: Princess Books, 2003), p. 4.

7. John Edward, *One Last Time* (New York: Berkley Books, 1999), p. 44.

8. Edward, *After Life*, p. xvi.

9. Ibid.

10. Edward, *One Last Time*, p. 44.

11. Cathy Hainer, "Lessons for Living Are Heaven-Sent," *USA Today*, March 19, 1998, Internet edition.

12. "TV Interview with James Van Praagh," *Larry King Live,* January 10, 2003, Internet transcript.

13. Susan King, "Messages from Beyond," *Los Angeles Times,* April 28, 2002, Internet edition.

14. Edward, *One Last Time,* p. 43.

15. Chris Ballard, "John Edward is the Oprah of the Other Side," *New York Times Magazine,* July 29, 2001, Internet edition.

16. John Edward, interview with *Teen People,* March 1, 2002, Internet edition.

17. Edward, *One Last Time,* pp. 45-46.

18. Ibid.

19. Ibid.

20. Ibid.

21. Ibid., p. 51.

22. Ibid., pp. 45-46.

23. Ibid.

24. Catherine Crier, "Interview with Psychic John Edward," *The Crier Report,* Fox News Network, May 26, 1999, Internet edition.

25. Edward, *One Last Time,* p. 78.

26. Ballard, "John Edward is the Oprah of the Other Side."

27. Sandra Barrera, "Self-described 'Ordinary Guy' John Edward Links the Living and the Dead for Those Who Believe," *Los Angeles Daily News,* September 3, 2002, Internet edition.

28. Michael Shermer, "Deconstructing the Dead," *Skeptic,* August 2001, Internet edition.

29. James Underdown, "They See Dead People—or Do They?" *Skeptical Inquirer,* September 1, 2003, Internet edition.

30. Marisa Guthrie, "Psychic John Edward Challenges Viewers to Believe the Dead Just Can't Shut up," *The Boston Herald,* August 24, 2001, Internet edition.

31. Kathy Cano Murillo, "Psychic Helps Others Discover Their Abilities," *The Arizona Republic,* May 9, 2005, Internet edition.

32. Char Margolis, *Questions from Earth, Answers from Heaven* (New York: St. Martin's, 2000), p. 106.

33. Sylvia Browne website.

34. "Psychic Browne Sees through the Skeptics," *Las Vegas Sun,* July 13, 2001, Internet edition.

35. James Walker, "The Psychics," *Watchman Expositor,* vol. 14, no. 2, Internet edition.

36. "The Truth About Uri Geller," *Time,* June 13, 1988, p. 72

37. Harry Houdini, *A Magician Among the Spirits* (Alexandria, VA: Time-Life Books, 1991), p. 270.

38. James Underdown, "They See Dead People—or Do They?"

39. Michael Shermer, "How Psychics and Mediums Work," in *How We Believe: The Search for God in an Age of Science,* (New York: W.H. Freeman, 1999), n.p.

40. Shermer, "How Psychics and Mediums Work."

41. Underdown, "They See Dead People—or Do They?"

42. Joe Nickell, "John Edward: Hustling the Bereaved," *Skeptical Inquirer,* November/December 2001, Internet edition.

43. Andre Kole and Terry Holley, *Astrology and Psychic Phenomena* (Grand Rapids: Zondervan, 1998), p. 15.

44. Kenneth Boa, *Cults, World Religions, and You* (Wheaton: Victor Books, 1986), pp. 133-34.

45. Walter Martin, *The Kingdom of the Cults* (Minneapolis: Bethany House Publishers, 2003), p. 268.

46. Martin, p. 263.

47. Marcia Montenegro, "I See Dead People," *Christian Research Journal,* vol. 25, no. 1, 2003, Internet edition.

CHAPTER 7—ASSESSING THE ACCURACY OF PSYCHIC MEDIUMS

1. "Exclusive Interview with James Van Praagh," *phenomeNEWS,* May 1, 2003, Internet edition.

2. "Exclusive Interview with James Van Praagh."

3. Bryan Farha, "Blundered Predictions in 2004," *Skeptical Inquirer,* March 1, 2005, Internet edition.

4. *Wikipedia,* s.v. "Sylvia Browne."

5. Roger Friedman, "TV Psychic Misses Mark on Miners," Fox News, January 5, 2006, Internet edition.

6. Shari Waxman, "Alleged Psychic John Edward Actually Gambles on Hope and Basic Laws of Statistics," *Salon,* June 13, 2002, Internet edition.

7. Michael Shermer, "Deconstructing the Dead," *Skeptic,* Internet edition.

8. Ibid.

9. John Edward, *Crossing Over* (New York: Princess Books, 2001), p. 245.

10. Ibid., p. 250.

11. "Interview With Char Margolis," *Larry King Live,* July 9, 2004, CNN transcript, Internet edition.

12. "A Herd of Psychics on Larry King," James Randi Educational Foundation website, March 9, 2001.

13. John Edward, *After Life* (New York: Princess Books, 2003), pp. 85-86.

14. James Van Praagh, *Talking to Heaven* (New York: Signet, 1997), p. 59.

15. Edward, *After Life,* pp. 85-86.

16. Waxman, "Alleged Psychic Actually Gambles."

17. Edward, *After Life,* p. 23.

18. Edward, *Crossing Over,* pp. 131-32.

19. Ibid.

20. Sylvia Browne, *The Other Side and Back* (New York: Signet, 2000), p. xxiii.

21. Bryan Farha, "Sylvia Browne TV Psychic Sidesteps Challenges," *Skeptical Inquirer,* November 1, 2003, Internet edition.

22. Sylvia Browne website.

23. *Wikipedia,* s.v. "Sylvia Browne."

24. Sylvia Browne website.

25. Marcia Montenegro, "The Psychics: Can They Help You?" CANA website, posted February 1, 2003.

CHAPTER 8—DOCTRINES OF DEMONS

1. Sylvia Browne, *Life on the Other Side* (New York: Signet, 2000), p. 38.

2. Norman Geisler, *Explaining Hermeneutics* (Oakland: International Council on Biblical Inerrancy 1983), p. 7.

3. Gordon Lewis, *Confronting the Cults* (Phillipsburg, NJ: Presbyterian & Reformed, 1985), p. 137.

4. Browne, *Life on the Other Side,* p. 41.

5. Robin Westin, *Channelers: A New Age Directory* (New York: Putnam, 1988), pp. 91-93.

6. Cited in Irvine Robertson, *What the Cults Believe* (Chicago: Moody Press, 1983), p. 152.

7. Sylvia Browne with Lindsay Harrison, *Phenomenon* (New York: Dutton, 2005), p. 42.

8. Norman Geisler, *Christian Apologetics* (Grand Rapids: Baker, 1978), p. 187.

9. Walter Martin, *The Kingdom of the Cults* (Minneapolis: Bethany House, 2003), p. 289.

10. Van Praagh, *Talking to Heaven* (New York: Signet, 1997), pp. 42-43.

11. Norman Geisler, Ronald Brooks, *Christianity Under Attack* (Dallas: Quest, 1985), p. 43.

12. Helen Schucman, *A Course in Miracles* (New York: Foundation for Inner Peace, 1992), 1:375.

13. Jane Roberts, *Seth Speaks* (New York: Prentice Hall, 1972), p. 89.

14. Ramtha with D.J. Mahr, *Voyage to the New World* (New York: Faucett, 1987), pp. 130, 149.

15. Schucman, 1:32-33.

CHAPTER 9—THE TRUTH ABOUT THE AFTERLIFE

1. Sylvia Browne, *Life on the Other Side* (New York: Signet, 2000), p. 51.

2. "An Interview with Psychic and Medium James Van Praagh," *Mysteries Magazine,* January 1, 2005, Internet edition.

3. Review of *Talking to Heaven,* by James Van Praagh. *Publishers Weekly,* October 27, 1999, Internet edition.

4. "An Interview with Psychic and Medium James Van Praagh."

5. *Wikipedia,* s.v. "Sylvia Browne.

6. Browne, *Life on the Other Side,* p. 95.

7. Sylvia Browne with Lindsay Harrison, *Phenomenon* (New York: Dutton, 2005), p. 204.

8. James Van Praagh, *Talking to Heaven* (New York: Signet, 1997), p. 44.

9. Dru Sefton, "Van Praagh: Steering the Mediumship," *Kansas City Star,* May 17, 1998, Internet edition.

10. "An Interview with Psychic and Medium James Van Praagh."

11. Cathy Hainer, "Lessons for Living Are Heaven-Sent," *USA Today,* March 19, 1998, Internet edition.

12. Char Margolis, *Questions from Earth, Answers from Heaven* (New York: St. Martin's, 2000), p. 54.

13. "I Have Proof There Is Life After Death, Clairvoyant Claims," *San Antonio Express-News,* June 14, 1998, Internet edition.

14. Sylvia Browne, *The Other Side and Back* (New York: Signet, 2000), p. 24.

15. Browne, *Life on the Other Side,* p. 122.

16. "An Interview with Psychic and Medium James Van Praagh."

17. Van Praagh, *Talking to Heaven,* p. 104.

18. James Van Praagh, *Heaven and Earth* (New York: Pocket Books, 2001), p. 183.

19. John Edward, *One Last Time* (New York: Berkley Books, 1999), pp. 158-59.

20. Van Praagh, *Heaven and Earth,* p. 126.

21. Browne, *Life on the Other Side,* p. 198.

22. Ibid., p. 207.

23. Ibid., p. 218.

CHAPTER 10—SHARPENING DISCERNMENT ON PSYCHIC MEDIUMS

1. Stafford Wright, *Christianity and the Occult* (Chicago: Moody Press, 1971), p. 112.

2. Marcia Montenegro, "The Psychics: Can They Help You?" CANA website, posted February 1, 2003.

3. Kevin Christopher, "Medium John Edward Hosts Sci-Fi Cable Show," *Skeptical Inquirer,* September 1, 2000, Internet edition.

4. Kenneth Boa, *Cults, World Religions, and You* (Wheaton: Victor Books, 1986), p. 163.

5. James Hassett, "Caution: Meditation Can Hurt," *Psychology Today,* November 1978, pp. 125-26.

6. Cited in Vishal Mangalwadi, *When the New Age Gets Old* (Downers Grove: Inter-Varsity Press, 1993), p. 82.

7. Ibid., p. 81.

8. Cited in Josh McDowell and Don Stewart, *Answers to Tough Questions* (Nashville: Nelson, 1994), p. 83.

9. "John Edward: Psychic Phenomenon," *People Weekly,* December 31, 2001, Internet edition.

POSTSCRIPT

1. The Barna Group, "New Research Explores Teenage Views and Behavior Regarding the Supernatural," January 23, 2006, Internet edition; Roxana Hadadi, "Do You Believe In Ghosts?" *Diamondback Online News,* February 3, 2006, Internet edition; *Wikipedia,* s.v. "Parapsychology;" Pauline Chiou, "Listening to the Voices of Ghosts," CBS News, February 3, 2006.

2. Sylvia Browne website.

BIBLIOGRAPHY

Abanes, Richard. *Cults, New Religious Movements, and Your Family.* Wheaton, IL: Crossway, 1998.

Ankerberg, John, and John Weldon. *Cult Watch.* Eugene, OR: Harvest House Publishers, 1991.

Boa, Kenneth. *Cults, World Religions, and You.* Wheaton, IL: Victor Books, 1986.

Browne, Sylvia. *Life on the Other Side: A Psychic's Tour of the Afterlife.* New York: Signet, 2001.

————. *The Other Side and Back: A Psychic's Guide to Our World and Beyond.* New York: Signet, 2000.

————. *Phenomenon: Everything You Need to Know About the Paranormal.* New York: Dutton, 2005.

Denning, Hazel M. *Hauntings! Real-Life Encounters with Troubled Spirits.* New York: Barnes & Noble, 1996.

Edward, John. *After Life: Answers from the Other Side.* New York: Princess Books, 2003.

————. *Crossing Over.* New York: Princess Books, 2001.

————. *One Last Time: A Psychic Medium Speaks to Those We Have Loved and Lost.* New York: Berkley Books, 1999.

I Never Believed in Ghosts Until...100 Real-Life Encounters. Collected by the editors of *USA Weekend.* Chicago: Contemporary Books, 1992.

Koch, Kurt. *Between Christ and Satan.* Grand Rapids: Kregel Publications, 1972.

————. *Occult ABC.* Grand Rapids: Kregel, Publications 1986.

————. *Occult Bondage and Deliverance.* Grand Rapids: Kregel Publications, 1972.

Margolis, Char. *Questions from Earth, Answers from Heaven.* New York: St. Martin's, 2000.

Martin, Walter. *The Kingdom of the Cults.* Minneapolis: Bethany House, 2003.

Parker, Russ. *Battling the Occult.* Downers Grove, IL: InterVarsity Press, 1990.

Rhodes, Ron. *The Challenge of the Cults and New Religions.* Grand Rapids: Zondervan, 2003.

————. *Find It Quick Handbook on Cults and New Religions.* Eugene, OR: Harvest House Publishers, 2005.

————. *The New Age Movement.* Grand Rapids: Zondervan, 2001.

Roberts, Nancy. *Haunted Houses: Chilling Tales from 24 American Homes.* Guilford, CT: The Globe Pequot Press, 1998.

Robertson, Irvine. *What the Cults Believe.* Chicago: Moody Press, 1983.

Rule, Leslie. *Coast to Coast Ghosts: True Stories of Hauntings Across America.* Kansas City: Andrews McMeel Publishing, 2001.

————. *Ghosts Among Us: True Stories of Spirit Encounters.* Kansas City: Andrews McMeel Publishing, 2004.

Ryerson, Kevin, and Stephanie Harolde. *Spirit Communication.* New York: Bantam, 1989.

Swenson, Orville. *The Perilous Path of Cultism.* Caronport, SK: Briercrest Books, 1987.

Van Praagh, James. *Heaven and Earth: Making the Psychic Connection.* New York: Pocket Books, 2001.

————. *Talking to Heaven: A Medium's Message of Life After Death.* New York: Signet, 1997.

If you have any questions or comments, feel free to
contact Reasoning from the Scriptures Ministries.

RON RHODES
Reasoning from the Scriptures Ministries

PHONE: 214-618-0912
EMAIL: ronrhodes@earthlink.net
WEB: www.ronrhodes.org

Free newsletter available upon request

Other Great Harvest House Reading
by Ron Rhodes

Find It Quick Handbook on Cults and New Religions
This concise handbook catalogs 40 groups. The brief examinations of each group includes a short history of the sect or new religion, an explanation of the group's major doctrines, and the Christian apologetic response.

Find It Fast in the Bible
A quick reference that lives up to its name! With more than 400 topics and 8,000-plus references, this comprehensive, topical guide provides one-line summaries of each verse. Perfect for research, discussions, and Bible studies.

~

The 10 Things You Should Know About the Creation vs. Evolution Debate
This helpful guide demonstrates why the two sides of the debate are mutually exclusive. You will deepen your appreciation for the wonder of creation and see how it points to the reality of the Creator.

The 10 Most Important Things You Can Say to a Catholic
If you want to witness to Catholic friends or be more informed about their beliefs, you'll appreciate this fact-filled addition to the popular series. It discusses use of the Apocrypha, the role of tradition, purgatory, and Mary worship.

The 10 Most Important Things You Can Say to a Jehovah's Witness
Essential information for effectively witnessing to Jehovah's Witnesses. Includes a look at errors in the New World Translation Bible, false prophecies of the sect's leaders, and their unbiblical views. Great for Bible studies, youth groups.

The 10 Most Important Things You Can Say to a Mormon
For Christians witnessing to Mormons, this is a must-have, covering the Mormon view of the Bible and the Book of Mormon's origins. Stresses the importance of the Trinity, salvation by grace not works, and more.

~

Reasoning from the Scriptures with Muslims
Who was Muhammad? What kind of inspiration and authority does the Quran have? How can Muslims be reached with the good news? Each chapter examines a Muslim belief and compares it with biblical Christianity.

Reasoning from the Scriptures with Catholics
This thorough, easy-to-use reference examines Catholic beliefs and practices and outlines verses typically cited to support those views. A must-have tool for sharing the good news of salvation by faith alone with Catholics.

Reasoning from the Scriptures with the Mormons
Powerful tools for sharing the truth of God's Word in a loving and gracious way are presented in a simple, step-by-step format.

Reasoning from the Scriptures with the Jehovah's Witnesses
Many outstanding features make this the *complete* hands-on guide to sharing the truth of God's Word in a loving, gracious way. Includes favorite tactics used by the Witnesses and effective biblical responses.

∼

The Complete Guide to Christian Denominations
Ron Rhodes has compiled his extensive research into a handy, easy-to-use manual that provides accurate, straightforward information about various churches. Includes each denomination's brief history, its most important doctrinal beliefs, and distinctive teachings.

The Complete Book of Bible Promises
Bible promise books abound—but not like this one! Two hundred alphabetized categories of verses include explanatory headings, insights from the original languages, and deeply moving quotes from famous Christian authors and hymns.

∼

Quick Reference Guides
In 16 pages of concise, reader-friendly information, these booklets present the major points and arguments of the religion or subject discussed. Side-by-side comparisons with biblical teachings are provided for a scriptural perspective. Ideal for at-a-glance reference or for giving away.
  • *Believing in Jesus: What You Need to Know*
  • *Islam: What You Need to Know*
  • *Jehovah's Witnesses: What You Need to Know*

∼

Why Do Bad Things Happen If God Is Good?
Bible scholar Ron Rhodes addresses the problem of pain with the heart of a pastor and the mind of an apologist. Ron explores the unshakable biblical truths that provide a strong foundation in stormy times.

Angels Among Us

What are angels like? What do they do? Are they active today? Taking you on a fascinating and highly inspirational tour of God's Word, Ron provides solid, biblically based answers to these questions and more.

Understanding the Bible from A to Z

An encyclopedia that is compact enough to be quick and easy to use, this handy reference includes only the topics that you will want and only the vital information you will need.